My Father the Godfather

By Daryl Brown and Michael P. Chabries

Through the eyes of the son.

Brown-Chabries/My Father the Godfather

Published by Waldorf Publishing
2140 Hall Johnson Road
#102-113
Grapevine, Texas 76051
www.WaldorfPublishing.com
www.MyFathertheGodfather.com

My Father the Godfather
Second Edition
ISBN 9781633150829

Copyright © 2014

All rights reserved. No part of this book may be reproduced or transmitted in any form or by any means whatsoever without express written permission from the author, except in the case of brief quotations embodied in critical articles and reviews. Please refer all pertinent questions to the publisher. All rights reserved. No part of this book may be reproduced or transmitted in any form or by any means, electronic or mechanical, including photocopying, recording, or by an information storage and retrieval system, except by a reviewer who may quote brief passages in a review to be printed in a magazine or newspaper, without permission in writing from the publisher.

Dedication

I would like to thank my spiritual guide Brother Amun for guiding me on the right path, love you. I would like to thank Freddie Simonson (Rasul) my best friend for dreaming with me, love you. I would like to thank my photographer Sam Coles for being there for me when I really needed him, love you. Last but not least my sister Linda Boyce, I do not know what I would have done without you, I love you. I would like to dedicate this book to my mother Beatrice Ford Stokes (RIP) I miss you so much.
Daryl Brown

This book is dedicated to those who live their lives for good.
Michael P. Chabries

Brown-Chabries/My Father the Godfather

Section I
My Father - The Godfather

Black-assed nigger!

My father left his majestic fingerprints all over the world, but to his wife, Adrienne Brown, he was often called a "black-assed nigger."

He was affectionately known as The Godfather of Soul; Soul Brother Number One; Mr. Please, Please, Please; The Hardest Working Man in Show Business; The Sex Machine and Mr. Dynamite. But to me, he was daddy.

My father was a man of contradictions. He was born dead! Contradictions continued from his birth on May 3, 1933, until his death in 2006. Simply stated; he filled stadiums, stopped riots, caused wars to cease, furthered civil rights, revolutionized modern music, changed the entertainment industry, financially saved families and was adored by hundreds of millions of people, yet was a lonely man who lost many personal wars to inner-demons.

Scandal sells. Misrepresentations in movies, books, and magazines make for salacious stories and high profits, each failing to capture the truth of James Brown. Perhaps the truth was never the purpose. Perhaps James Brown was little more than a commodity.

Brown was exceptionally brilliant, unbelievably kind, generous to a fault, a musical talent without peer, a shrewd businessman, political genius and a prude when it came to

5

profanity and married women. That side of Brown is not just overlooked; it is discarded as chaff in the wind.

George "Spike" Nealy, percussionist and friend, may have said it best: "Negative sells regarding James Brown. It doesn't surprise me. It doesn't surprise me at all. But if you are going to be fair about it you have to talk about everything good too. By the time you finish talking about everything good, the bad is nothing more than a drop of water in a bucket. It is just the way it was."

For those who share their stories in this book, he was much more.

Unlike other tales of Mr. James Brown, this is not a work of historical fiction. Assembled together are many in his inner circle - although there are others who have their own story to tell. Each member knew him for many years. His spouse, mistress, manager, employees, band members, doctor, friends, and confidants reveal their experiences with my father, James Joseph Brown.

Accounts often contradict one another; an indication of truth rather than corroboration. I was not afraid to include stories from people that share opposing views. They knew James Brown in a way that I did not. It is not the purpose of this book to enhance or undermine their words. For each, it is their sacred truth. I am grateful they have been willing to share.

This account of the life of James Brown is not intended to be a chronological journey from beginning to end.

Rather it begins with the bookend events of his life; the miraculous birth in Barnwell, South Carolina and the unexpected (and unexplained) death on Christmas Day. Each contributor carefully and thoughtfully added a piece to the perplexing puzzle of his life.

I will take you - we will take you - inside the Godfather. This journey will travel beyond sex, drugs, Soul, Funk, and R&B. The curtains will be drawn to provide a peek into the world of religion, politics, professional sports, racism, the entertainment industry, roots magic, and the murder of a child. People and events you may have thought were real - simply were not. You will see with clarity, a world of illusion that will leave your head shaking.

I hope you will laugh, cry, and feel the sense of sadness and anger that I continue to feel after my father's passing, as well as the indescribable joy having had James Brown as my father. He was more remarkable than I, or anyone, can express in words.

I miss him.

It may not be possible to convey the sole truth of James Brown. However, after reading from those in the inner-circle, you will begin to understand his soul truth.

Jump on this Night Train.
"All aboard!"

Barnwell to Augusta

When a legend is told over and over again, it becomes the truth - even when it isn't. Most can't believe the story my father told of his upbringing. I am here to tell you…It was worse.

South Carolina was slave country - some say it still is. My grandmother, Susie, worked in the fields all day stopping only long enough to have a baby. She wept hysterically; the baby was not breathing. Grandpa Joe waited outside the shack both dazed and confused.

My Aunt told me he was born with a veil over his face. I had no idea what that meant. Was it the afterbirth that covered him and stopped him from breathing, or something else? I don't know.

Charles Bobbit, his long-time manager and friend makes it clearer: "The veil…it was over the pupil of the eyes. Most people do not know about that. Black people down here know about that kind of thing."

What I do know is that rural South Carolina was - and still is - "Roots" country. Roots magic is a mixture of African, Christian, and voodoo traditions that focus on healing, conjuring, and spells. Some who practice Roots believe "the veil" was a sign of psychic abilities.

Yes, it's true, Great Aunt Minnie breathed life into my father after he lay lifeless for twenty minutes. He was born dead. Some say my father didn't come from zero - "he

8

came from less than zero." To say that they were poor would be inaccurate. They hoped to become poor. They had almost nothing to their name except a new baby boy, James Joseph Brown.

I have been to the slave quarters where my father was born. It was no more than a hut, now overgrown by trees and native plants with remnants of a brick fireplace. Scraps of metal and wood are all that remain. The nearest structure is a quarter mile down a barely visible path, a single room with a loft. Absent are amenities commonplace for more than a century: windows, doors, bathroom, indoor plumbing and electricity. In reality, it was little more than a leaky roof over their heads. It was years before my father ever knew the comfort of a warm bed and soft pillow.

As soon as he could be left alone - he was. To say he grew up playing with doodle bugs (for which he wrote an instrumental song) is but a slight exaggeration. As a young child he was left alone in the forest and fields with all the bugs, beasts, rodents, pests and snakes. In some sense these were his family.

Often, he found himself lost in the forest looking for loved ones in the dead of night. Winds howled songs of loneliness. Penetrating moonlight through overcast skies guided the wandering boy. Crickets unsuccessfully tried singing him to sleep. He exerted every ounce of energy necessary to stay awake from dusk to dawn. This practice stayed with him until the day he died. He desperately hoped someone he loved would return to his side. Rarely did this happen. He was always emotionally alone.

Grandfather's carefully crafted story of Grandmother's exodus, leaving the faithful husband and adoring child, is ridiculous. Grandpa Joe raped and beat the hell out of Susie. He beat her badly, just like he did many other women over the years. Both drank corn liquor and whiskey, all the stuff that could kill you. They would lose their minds. Both were feisty when they were young, although they mellowed with age.

One night, grandfather returned to the shack more angry and violent than usual. The yelling started, then came the beating, but this time grandmother grabbed her little boy and started to run down the dirt road adjacent to the cotton fields where she worked. Both were dressed in little more than rags.

Susie had my father in her arms, holding him tight. Grandfather pulled out his gun and started firing. She froze. Grandma told me years later she 'knew in her mind' if she didn't leave the child, they were both going to get killed. She placed him down on the ground and sent him back to his father. Her eyes were filled with terror. Fear coursed through her veins. Her heart was beating so fast she could barely breathe, but she started to run again - stumbling down the road as tears blinded her eyes. She never looked back. It was too painful.

Vicki Anderson, the wife of Bobby Byrd said: "Susie did not leave the child and her husband the way it has been portrayed in the media. That is not so. That is so far from being the truth. Of course, I wasn't there when James was born. But I was told along with Deidre Jenkins, the mother of James' oldest daughters, Deanna and Yamma. She begged me to tell her children. Deidre said, 'James will forever beat women until he finds out the truth.' His mother did not give him away. I'm telling you, that is a fact. Joe was shooting at her. She said to Joe, 'Let me take my child.' People who are telling the lies are just talking to get a penny. The people don't want to hear lies. They want to hear REAL things."

The legendary story told of my grandmother willingly walking away from a helpless husband and loving child is little more than the images my father grew up with before memories can be fully formed. Young James was a boy trying to honor the tales of the only parent he knew. Joe never told his son the truth of their tumultuous history. He continued to degrade Susie as justification for his own hatred and behavior toward women.

The story haunted, crippled, and defined my father his entire life. Every person close to him heard the tragedy of his momma leaving him alone in Barnwell. He never let the pain go. His pain penetrated his music. His Please, Please, Please, at the end of every performance was grounded in this perpetual turmoil.

11

Despite my grandfather's cruelty, James Joseph Brown loved his daddy. Sadly, I have come to know firsthand what it is like to love someone so flawed.

My father saw it all. He heard it all. Yet, he dutifully protected the tragic legacy of his parents. It would be accurate to say that James Brown was abandoned long before his mother left for good. He felt abandoned his entire life. That was the most real thing he felt.

Some of my father's friends believe that his sense of aloneness began when his mother abandoned him at the age of four. They told me James did give $25,000 to the nursing home where Susie was being cared for, but he really didn't respect her, and he certainly didn't forgive her. I think they were wrong. What they did understand correctly, was my father was very close to Mr. Joseph Brown, his father.

Joseph Brown was born on March 27, 1912, and passed away on July 10, 1993. He was the son of James and Mary Alice Gardner.

"Pops" is how I knew him. As a young man, Pops was angry, he was a drunk, and he was rarely home to care for the child. When he returned to the house he was known to be rough, beating his little boy if he ever stepped out of line and even if he didn't.

Pops loved to gamble. The legend of Joe Brown is told in family circles. If he thought you were cheating at cards or any other game of chance, he would pull out his gun and shoot you. He didn't need an explanation - he only had to be suspicious.

My father inherited Joe's penchant for fairness. If he suspected shaved dice or a fixed game, he would turn the table upside down. Papa Don't Take No Mess was written in 1974 about my grandfather. The lyrics are descriptive and chilling.

Papa digs the chick
If she look real slick
Papa didn't cuss
He didn't raise a whole lotta fuss
But when we did wrong
Papa beat the hell out of us

"Papa beat the hell out of us." For my father, a good beating was to be silently endured. Silence was a sign of manhood. Another sign of masculinity was promiscuous women rotating through a man's bed like an amusement park's carousel in summertime. Get on, get in, and get off. After all, "Papa digs the chick if she looks real slick."

The Great Depression impoverished many Americans. For a black man in the South, it was devastating. Was it any wonder James Brown had flour-sacks sewn together for underwear, and a father always trying to hustle his next nickel? Walking to find his family while barely clothed was commonplace for my dad. Economic hardship drove my father, at a tender age, to walk more than 50 miles from Barnwell, South Carolina to Augusta, Georgia to stay with family. Young James had no shoes; the roads were dirt. Ironically, the man who made famous Get Up On The Good Foot, started life barefoot.

Eventually, he called Augusta home.

Thankfully for my father, World War II arrived just in time. Lonely soldiers looking for ladies, a game of dice, and quick entertainment were the perfect training ground for the boy with a burgeoning entrepreneurial vision.

Twiggs Street - 944 to be exact - was the location of Aunt Honey's home. "Aunt Honey" was a perfect description for this business woman. What she had to offer was sweet and went down easy. Home, brothel, house of ill repute…all semantics. It was a whorehouse with a long supply of testosterone-laden young men looking to drop a few bucks. Attention needed to be diverted from the very real possibility of a bullet to their head during deployment.

Prohibition provided the perfect opportunity to produce and profit from whiskey, corn liquor, or a smooth glass of moonshine - if "shine" can ever be described as smooth. A drink here satisfied the thirst of future war heroes. Boys became men in Augusta.

Soldiers circled around my father to watch his soon-to-be famous footwork. James Brown was a prodigy, and he didn't even know the meaning of the word. Paying customers sensed he was destined to be spectacular. They were amazed by his dance moves and he was amazed by the look in their eyes. Brown never diverted his attention from the expressions of the soldiers. What could he do to make them reach deeper into their pockets and drop more coins in the hat? He was a supreme student, analyzing every detail of his audience. This is a practice he embraced his entire career.

James Brown became a master of taking care of his audience and feeding their insatiable appetites. Every performance had a crescendo and a climax. His energy was boundless. When finished, he simply moved to the next show, having left them fully satisfied. Money was scarce, but money was to be had. As long as he was in demand, he supplied. He raised more income than most adults in the family.

Buck dancing originated among African slaves. "The Shuffling Coon - Buck & Wing Dance - The Quaintest Dance Step Ever Conceived" was an 1800s tune with an unfortunate title. The score was written by John Phillip Sousa. Buck and wing dance incorporated solo steps off the floor combined with a straight, still torso. Emphasis is always on the dancer remaining on their toes rather than heels. If you can't remember James Brown, think of Michael or Usher. They were inspired by Brown. In his prime - James Brown had no equal.

Understanding the whorehouse is critical to comprehend James Brown's view of women. Women were objects to satisfy men's desire. "It's a Man's Man's Man's World" after all. He came to those distorted conceptions of human relationships honestly. Whatever sermon was preached on Sunday could never counteract the sermon he saw each and every day. Imagine the screaming homily he heard every night in a home filled with whores! Combined with his issues of abandonment, is it any wonder he developed an insatiable desire for sex? Copulation was hardwired into his mind during his formative years.

"The Terry" was a neighborhood on the wrong side of the Augusta tracks. It was defined by violent crime. Primarily populated by black citizens guns and knives were the weapons of choice. My father became proficient with both. These were tough people living on the wrong side of survival. My father learned to box and fight with reckless abandon. Though I am much larger than my father, I always knew he could whip my ass if I ever crossed the line.

In Augusta, my father learned of government corruption: people consume alcohol, the government prohibits the sale of alcohol, officials accept bribes to look the other way. How could he conclude anything other than the government in practice is little more than 'legal' extortion?

Theft is theft. He never trusted government officials, and he never trusted law enforcement. If you were black and engaged in illegal distribution of alcohol and prostitution, the cost of doing business was significantly higher than your white counterpart. Segregation clearly extended to fines, jail sentences, and bribes. Aunt Honey paid off more than her share of police and government officials just to maintain a meager existence.

If the government could steal without penalty, why shouldn't Brown? Dad just followed their lead. He would steal anything he could get his hands on. His behavior had a consequence. When dad was about 15 years old, an ambitious solicitor tried to shut down the crooks inside the government. He failed in his prosecution. The red-faced solicitor turned his attention to a petty thief. Putting away "a nigger" would gain favor with Augusta money.

My father was sentenced to 16 years of hard labor for stealing less than $250.00.

Buddy Dallas observed: "The consequences of segregation influenced Mr. Brown in such a way that he could never let go of the past. Segregation affected Mr. Brown in the most profound way. Segregation left Mr. Brown perpetually in a survival mode. He always carried that burden with him."

Living in survival mode makes for a lifetime of bad decisions.

William Murrell was my father's personal driver in the last decade of his life. His story illustrates the sadness my father carried to his grave: "He didn't talk about growing up too much. I took him by the house one time. Man, you talk about a shack. It didn't have no floors in it. I'm talking dirt. This man came from minus zero. Nobody grows up like this man. I'm saying, you sleeping with the bugs. Dirt floor. Two-room shack. It was pitiful man. When the wind blows, you feel it. It was common in the house to have a woodstove for heat. You had to cut wood to keep the house warm.

It took me 45 minutes to drive there. It's in a little place called Snellville, right next to Barnwell, South Carolina. His house is near the fork in the road. It's almost gone now.

He would walk from that house to Augusta. He would stay right over there on Seventh Street. Soldiers would pitch him money to dance. He would perform for them. It's at least a 50 mile walk. He would walk all the way as a kid. I don't know how long it took him to get here. That's what he told me. He would hitchhike sometimes and walk.

I met some of his kinfolk. I took him over to Twiggs Street where he told me that he would rob and steal. He would run down this little tunnel to hide. It's a nice little area now, but it wasn't back then. He would hide stuff in the tunnel. He had a little warehouse over there. Him and his partner, "Big Boy" would steal things and hide in there. His partner is still alive. I've taken them over there many times. They would talk about old times and all of that good stuff.

He was a boxer before he was an entertainer. He was the baddest. He was the fastest boxer; fast with his hands, fast with his feet. That's why he could do the splits and dance so fast. He learned from boxing."

My grandfather is buried in Augusta - nowhere near my father. The copper top on his gravesite says the following:

HE WAS A NATIVE OF BARNWELL, SOUTH CAROLINA AND THE SON OF THE LATE JAMES AND MARY ALICE GARDNER.
HE SERVED IN THE UNITED STATES NAVY IN WORLD WAR II AND THE KOREAN WAR.
HE IS THE FATHER OF WORLD RENOWNED ENTERTAINER, JAMES BROWN.
WITH ONLY A SECOND GRADE EDUCATION, MR. BROWN WORKED HARD. ONE NIGHT HE WAS FACED WITH TAKING HIS LIFE SAVINGS IN A SNUFF CAN AND ESCAPING A SLAVESHIP IN BARNWELL, SOUTH CAROLINA, TO FIND BETTER WORK IN AUGUSTA, GEORGIA SO THAT HE COULD SUPPORT HIS FAMILY. HE WORKED IN A FURNITURE STORE WHERE HE MADE SEVEN DOLLARS A WEEK. HE ONCE BROUGHT HOME AN ORGAN WITH A BROKEN LEG, WHICH SPARKED YOUNG JAMES BROWN TO BEGIN PLAYING MUSIC.

WHEN THE FAMILY TOOL ILL HE WOULD WALK
SEVENTEEN MILES TO TOWN FOR FOOD TO KEEP
FROM BORROWING FLOUR FROM NEIGHBORS.

WE LOVE YOU "POP"
JAMES BROWN

Prelude to Death

Crack, pneumonia, congestive heart failure, cancer or murder?

Take your pick.

Those that were closest to him don't agree. The evidence is buried. Traces may exist with the body.

Curiously, an autopsy was never performed.

These are several of the accounts from those who worked with him prior to his death.

My father actually believed that when you died, you were not really dead. He believed that you are in a deep sleep or a zombielike state. He believed that. He REALLY believed that. He told many people around him the same thing, including those in his office and Tomi Rae.

He told me that when he died there were certain things that he wanted to be buried with. During the time I was with him, certain things could not be done because the technology simply did not exist. He wanted to be buried with a video camera in the coffin. He wanted oxygen tanks that had an endless supply of oxygen. He wanted his cell phone with a battery that would never run out. I laughed at him. I wanted to buy stock in that company.

He was so serious about these items in the coffin. Even more incredibly he wanted everyone at home to have their television focused on his dead/live/sleeping body, so when he did wake up, we could come and get him. He wanted to be sure that he was not embalmed. Of course, that was the first thing that happened.

He was very serious about these requests.

***

George "Spike" Nealy II – Percussionist and Friend

When we came off the stage in Russia during that very last run, it was freezing cold. It was snowing outside. I suspect that was probably when he caught pneumonia. He had his shirt open. This was not common. He usually stayed in the dressing room for at least two hours. He spent time under the hair dryer because he sweats so much. But that series of shows we couldn't spend any extra time. Our schedule was so tight - we had so many shows. We had to be back at the private plane and take off and move on. As we were leaving, I took my scarf and wrapped it around his neck.

I said to him, "Mr. Brown, you got to keep this around your neck, because, if you get sick - then that's it for us."

He said, "Son, now, I be alright."

I said "No, no, no. Take my scarf. I get another scarf. Take mine."

Mr. Brown said, 'Thank-you son, thank-you so much.'

We drove Mr. Brown to the airport the next morning. As we boarding the plane and walking down the aisle, he said, "Mr. Nealy, here's your scarf."

I told him no. "Mr. Brown, we are not through with this tour. I want you to keep this scarf. I will buy another scarf - I will buy me another one. Mr. Brown, if you stop, we stop."

It was too fast for him to leave. With his immune system already down due to the thirteen or fourteen shows we had performed nonstop. There was no time to rest. When you are dealing with the elements such as cold weather - it was just too much. If it was too much at our age, imagine what it did to a man who was 72?

***

<u>Hollie Farris</u> – Trumpet player and band director

Toward the end of his life we would hope to have a day in between shows. It didn't work out that way. However, he would always perform. We would perform three or four nights in a row. I have seen him do that over and over again. Nobody knew how he did it.

We never really knew how sick he was. He would never tell us. We could see him diminishing in strength over the last two years (of his life). We would go on the road and he would get perky as long as he was performing. After three weeks, we would go home and then he would rapidly decline. He would get unhealthy again (drugs).

The last six months of his life he started to lose significant weight. We could tell something was going on, but he would never talk about it. He continued to perform.

The next to the last show we ever performed was in Czechoslovakia. He performed one of the best shows that I had ever seen in 24 years. He only performed one more show after that. He died shortly thereafter. Many of the band members talked to me about the performance in Czechoslovakia. It was truly amazing. We talked about how great a show it was.

And then he died.

I don't know if he had a premonition that he was going to die, but that show was one of the very best ever. We had no idea how sick he was - he was in bad shape. But he had iron will. You can ask anyone who performed in the band and saw him during that performance. They will tell you. It was nothing short of miraculous. His last show was in Croatia. Then it was over.

I remember the day he died. I was asleep in my bed on Christmas morning. Someone called and asked me if I had heard the news? They said, "James died!" I could not believe it. We were supposed to go out on tour the very next day! The tour was going to last an entire month.

It is important to understand - when James Brown was on the road he would get healthy. When he got home, he would get unhealthy. Do you know what I mean?

After his performance in Croatia we had almost two months off. That is way too long for James Brown to be home. He could not come back from such a long stay at home. He would go home and not eat right. He would take too many drugs. His wife was not there to take care of them. He didn't have people close to him to take care of him. In previous years we had always been able to save

him. We would get him out on the road and get him right -
get him healthy. His reason for living returned. He became
excited again. He had things to do.

***

<u>Buddy Dallas</u> – Attorney & Friend

I was not with Mr. Brown when he died. I received a
phone call at 1:20 AM. Charles Bobbit was by his bed. Mr.
Washington was the caretaker of his house and was also
with him. Andre Moses White, a personal friend and
former Tampa Bay Buccaneer had been with him until
about 10:30 PM. Something happened to him during that
period of time. Mr. White said that he was fine and looking
forward to performing in Toronto on New Year's Eve.

I do believe that Mr. Brown had a premonition before
he passed. He died on the 25th of December. On the
Tuesday of that week I got a call from Mr. Brown. We
chatted and then he took on a serious tone. This is after I
had talked with him about walking with the graduating
class the following May, to receive an honorary doctorate
degree. I said to him, "Mr. Brown, I've been calling you
Mr. all these many years. I think it's ridiculous. I'm not
going call you that anymore."

"What is that you say Mr. Dallas?"

I said, "I'm not going call you Mr. Brown anymore.
It's Dr. Brown!"

It was December 10, 2006, that I called Mr. Brown.
We always referred to each other as Mr. Brown or Mr.

25

Dallas. He always used titles out of respect. It was the way James Brown was raised. I called him because I had been working with Dr. Lewis at the Paine College. I called him because I was suggesting that he receive an honorary doctorate. I believe he should have been recognized academically. What man had made a greater contribution to music? We had been working on this award for some time.

Just before he died, he participated in the toy giveaways for the children. He was in no way physically able to do that. He should've been in the hospital. However, he would not leave Augusta, Georgia until he took care of the children. He had just given away a trailer full of turkeys a few weeks earlier. Giving had become such a part of his life. He thoroughly enjoyed giving to others. People would line up for blocks to get a turkey. You just had to be there to get the feel, to experience the joy that he felt.

On Tuesday evening prior to his death on the 25th, he called. He was very relaxed. He was very subdued. We started to talk. He reminisced about so many things, many that I had not thought about in years. For example he said to me, "Mr. Dallas, you remember when you went to the bank for me? Mr. Dallas, you did not have to do that for me. But I thank you. I just want you to know, Mr. Dallas; I appreciate the things you have done for me."

The conversation lasted about 45 minutes. I commented to my wife that I wish they would have recorded our call. I knew he had always appreciated me. However, as I look back at it, I know he was telling me goodbye.

***

<u>David Cannon</u> – Accountant and Friend

This (conflict between parties) all started because Mr. Brown did not want to give the children, his children, the estate. He wanted to give them some of his personal effects, things around the house. He told them at Thanksgiving, the month before he died in December. He told them they were not going to get what they thought, and not to depend on him for money. He didn't give it to them when he was alive. They could not even come to his house without an appointment.

I was the one who introduced him to the attorneys to set up the trust. I saw that he wasn't giving his children anything.

"Mr. Brown,' I said to him, 'you've got to give something to your children."

"Mr. Cannon, I'm not going to do it."

"Mr. Brown, it just bothers me."

"Mr. Cannon, I know you're a good man. I know you are going to try to do something for those children. Don't you do anything until after I'm dead."

That was a conversation we had about six months before he died. After he died I went to the children with Buddy Dallas. I tried to explain to them how a charitable

27

trust would work. I told him what had to be done. I reminded them that their dad did not want them to have anything. I told them, however, that I could make them associates of the trust. They can be called advisors or some other kind of title. I was going to pay them $100,000 each year for the rest of their lives. The attorneys for the children rejected that. They said that they should each get millions of dollars from the trust. They removed me and Buddy Dallas so they could get to the money. Not surprisingly, the money is going to the attorneys and not the children.

Shortly before James Brown died, they dedicated and renamed the auditorium in Augusta, Georgia with his name. Mr. Brown thought he was going to have a little fun with me. I was standing at the side of the stage. With everyone in attendance he pointed over to me and said, "This is Mr. David Cannon." He said, "Mr. Cannon is hiding like he always does."

He wanted me to come up and say a few words. Of course I thanked the people and we were grateful the street was named after him as well. Mr. Brown thought it was funny that I was speaking. I'm sure that it was.

I was with Mr. Brown just a few minutes before he died. I was there, Mr. Bobbit was there, and Mr. Washington was on the way. He made me go home. I was sitting there in his hospital room and he said to me, "Mr. Cannon, you need to go home. It's Christmas Eve. I know you got family. I know you have grandchildren. Please go home."

I was sitting there with him in the room and it never occurred to me he could possibly die. I knew he was sick. Before I arrived in my house, Mr. Bobbit called to tell me that James Brown had died. Mr. Bobbit was there when I left - Mr. Washington was on his way to the hospital.

I did not suspect his condition was terminal. The doctors did not suspect so either. They told me that his passing was unexpected. He and I were talking about what his plans would be for Christmas and New Year's. We were talking about all of our plans as well as all of the business issues that we needed to address. I told him that we didn't need to worry about all of that right now; all we needed was to take care of him and get him out of the hospital. He ignored me and started talking business.

I do not have any knowledge of any wrongdoing regarding Mr. Brown's death. I don't know who would've gotten into the room to do it. I returned to the hospital Christmas morning and spoke with the doctor. He told me he did not expect Mr. Brown to die. The doctor wanted to perform an autopsy. I told him that I was not able to authorize the autopsy. It was never done.

I was never able to mourn his death. I received a phone call from Tomi Rae two hours after he died. The house was locked up tight. She had a press conference right at the gates - crying her eyes out. We have not had a moment's rest since that time.

***

<u>William Murrell</u> – **Personal Driver**

On 22 December, 2006, I saw James Brown for the last time. I called Minnesota Fattz from the radio station. It was Minnesota Fattz that James Brown adopted as his step son. I called Minnesota and I said, "Fattz, Mr. Brown is not going to be here very long. His skin looks silver."

I have never seen a silver person in my life before that day.

It was December 22, 2006, that I drove James Brown for the last time. He did not say one word. I said to myself, 'Something is wrong with this man.' He did not say one word from the time I picked him up, until the time I dropped him off. We would usually talk from the moment I picked him up to the time I dropped him off. We would talk about current events. He always asked me what was happening in Augusta. That day, he just sat in the back and looked around.

I kept looking in the rearview mirror and thinking that something was wrong with that man. I said,

"How are you doing Mr. Brown?"

Not one word. I said to myself, 'Wow. Something is wrong with this guy.'

I had picked him up before when he was intoxicated. In fact, I picked him up several times when he was high.

That day, it was just weird. His skin was silver. His whole complexion was gone. That was the day he did the public toy giveaway. The toy giveaway was at the Imperial Theatre in downtown Augusta, Georgia. He gave the toys out and took pictures with everybody that asked. He jumped in the car and I took him back home. He still did not say one word. It was different. It was very different

They - his inner circle - asked me to help take him to the dentist the very next day, the 23rd of December. I told them that I couldn't. I made a story that I needed to go shopping for my wife. I told them that I could not go out of town for that long. The truth is, I just couldn't stand to see him that way. I knew something was going to happen to him. I had a strong feeling. You know when you get the strong vibe, you have to go with your first impression. Three days after I had the impression, he was gone.

Remember, I worked in the hospital for 18 years. I have been around patients that died on me before they could even sign their name. I would admit patients to the hospital and ask them questions, and they would die right before my eyes - before we could even finish the paperwork. I had experienced this before. I recognized what was happening. That came into play. It was unreal.

***

<u>Vicki Anderson</u> – Wife of Bobby Byrd, Founder of the Famous Flames

We were friends to his death because I said 'No.' He really respected me for that. If you look at one of the biographies - the only singer you will see in the book is Vicki Anderson. His wife, Adrienne "Alphie" was in the book, but I was the only singer.

I know that just before he died he tried to call my husband and me four times. I have it on my phone. We were in church and the phone was on silent. We were in Church on Christmas Day. I did not know James was trying to call me. Charles Bobbit said, "Why didn't y'all try to return the call to James?" I told him that I never looked at my phone.

If he was going to repent to Bobby Byrd, that would have been a good time to do it. That was right before he died. We don't know what he really wanted with me and Bobby. He did not tell Charles Bobbit what he wanted with us. He died without asking forgiveness for the wrong he had done to Bobby and the things he did to me.

People only know James Brown the entertainer. He was the best in the world. He worked hard and he was a perfectionist. You couldn't do nothing half-way with him.

Charles Bobbit really loved James. Before James Brown died, Daryl was driving the four of us in the car. Brown said, "Charles Bobbit and Washington (the caretaker of his house) - I am going to take care of them."

He said that Tomi Rae should receive 17.5% of his estate. I thought that was an interesting number. The way the finances and the will have gone down, by golly!

He (Brown) said, "I will not leave a child of mine a dime! I am about children - young children. I have left them (the older children) stuff but it was not what they wanted."

We parked at a restaurant where Mr. Brown liked to eat when he was in Atlanta. We had taken him to the dentist. Charles Bobbit went to check out the restaurant to see if it was crowded. He wanted to make sure it was safe for Mr. Brown to enter. He didn't want the public to see James Brown in such a bad condition. Charles said,

"Vic, Mr. Brown looks too bad. I'm not going to take him in there."

He and Mr. Washington went in the restaurant and brought back a plate to go.

***

Charles Bobbit and Vicki Anderson

Charles Bobbit was present when Mr. Brown passed. Bobbit said: James Brown said, I didn't say that I was the closest one to him. I was with him most of the time. He opened up to me where he didn't open up to other people. I will tell you this…When he was hiring me he said, "I know we are going to be together until one of us died." Sadly, I was with him when he breathed his last breath. He (James Brown) was correct. Marva Whitney, one of his lead

33

singers, quoted Mr. Brown in her book: "There is a man coming and his name is Charles Bobbit. He is going to be with me until the very end."

I was happy and honored to know this man. He was a fantastic individual…We all have our demons. I will say this: I have never witnessed James Brown use drugs. I know that he did. I have seen him high - but he never let me see that. It was a strange thing that he would always tell me, "There are certain things that I will keep you out of because it is going to be trouble one of these days. I don't want you in the middle of it."

Vicki Anderson briefly stated, "Charles Bobbit was to receive a significant sum of money for the upcoming concerts he arranged."

Naturally, those payments never arrived.

***

My Thoughts

My father was murdered.

Two weeks before my father died I went to his house. The room smelled terrible. There was mess everywhere. Drugs. He was lying on the floor and his feet were swollen. I lifted my father up and put him on the bed.

He said, "Son, I'm glad you did this for me."

I told him he had to stop doing this. I told him that he couldn't smoke crack no more.

He said, "Son, I ain't smoking no crack."

I told him, "Dad, it's not going to be like that. I have a PhD in drug use. Don't lie to me. This will kill you."

At this time, I was like his father and he was like my son. I knew that my father ate too much salt. I knew that I needed to go get him some imitation salt. I knew that I needed to give him some water. He loves soda. He drank too much soda. I'm thinking of all of these issues he was dealing with - without talking to the doctor.

I returned to the home the next day. He told me that he was grateful I had helped him. He never talked to me like that before. Another week went by and I saw him on the day before Christmas Eve. He had been at it again. Drugs. He could hardly breathe. He was dehydrated. He had a leather jumpsuit on but he didn't have a shirt. He got out of the limousine and I knew something was wrong.

While we were visiting the doctor, they listened to his lungs. He was congested. The doctor asked him about his congestion. He told them, "I'm fine, I just need some water." Crack cocaine can cause congestion. The next week though, he was clean, no congestion.

I could not be with my father all day long. I had things to do. I had a family to take care of. I would call him every day to see how he was doing. He told me he was fine. When I called him the day before Christmas he was having a difficult time breathing.

He told the people that he was with he wanted to go home. I told him that we were going to try to get him to go to the hospital. He was gasping for air. He wouldn't go. I had to make a plan. We knew he was going to Dr. Reynolds for his teeth. We knew the Dentist could not work on him while he was sick and that he would get him to go to the hospital. I knew that my dad would not go to the hospital without a fight.

I was on my way to New Jersey. I called him. We talked for a long time. He sounded better. We talked for at least an hour and my father rarely talked for an hour. This was 23rd December, 2006. I was going home to New Jersey to stay with my mother. I stayed for the toy giveaway but then I left that night. He sounded better - but he was still sick. The trick was to get him to Dr. Reynolds office.

I was told that Andre White was there. Mr. Bobbit was there. Mr. Cannon was there. The doctor was there. He was completely clear. All of the drugs were out of him. They wanted him to stay one more day. I knew that we would have to cancel the first day of the concert tour. It was about 10 PM and everyone started to leave. The doctor was still there. The last man went downstairs to buy something for my father's stomach. He had indigestion. The pharmacy was closed. Half an hour later my father was dead. The doctor had no explanation.

Mr. Bobbit had called me that day. The doctors were aware of his drug use. I asked him, "Why are you telling me this?" I knew what he had done. I had to clean up the mess. Why would he mention that to me?

36

I was calling the hospital every hour on the hour. I was getting reports. I told one of my mother's friends that he had congestive heart failure and was smoking that damn crack. She mentioned something about him dying. Charles Bobbit told me again that they knew everything that he had done - talking about the drugs. I knew what he had done. So what?

I don't know what my father was trying to tell me. I had taken him to the hospital before when he was high on Angel dust. The hospital could clean him up. They had done it before. Nobody in the media needed to know. We kept it to ourselves. Half an hour later, the body was cold.

The doctor said he didn't know what happened. He said my father was up walking around. He was fine. He was joking. Mr. Washington would not leave my father's side. He is the caretaker at the house. It just seems strange to me that everybody said he was fine, and then all of a sudden he was dead.

Bobbit came to me after his death and said, "What is this I hear about an investigation? What is this I hear about murder?" I wondered why he was asking me all these questions. I wondered if he knew something. There were rumors going around. It didn't seem right.

Darren Chip Lumar was married to my sister Yamma. He went on television and said, "I am certain, I am positive, that Mr. Brown did not just die." Chip Lumar was killed. He was executed. A professional hit was placed on his head. He was killed because he went on television in Atlanta and told his story. It was a local affiliate. Lumar had $4000 on him. They didn't take it. It wasn't a robbery. It was a hit. They came to kill him.

I just have a gut feeling that he was killed.

Michael (Jackson) wanted out. He had risen to the top of the game. He knew his life was in jeopardy. I was not surprised that he died by an overdose administered by someone else's hands. When a celebrity or person in power no longer wants to cooperate, that is when your life is in jeopardy. My father's life was in jeopardy. Michael Jackson's life was in jeopardy.

The biggest threat to the establishment is when you no longer want to play by their rules and you get old. When you get older and you've made your money, you care less about what other people think. That is the case with my father. That is the case for Michael Jackson. That was the case for Elvis Presley. They know what a damaging game the entertainment industry can be. They don't want to see other people suffer.

***

Post Script

In July 2007, Darren Lumar provided an interview to Tony McNary of CBS Atlanta. He asked for a full investigation into James Brown's death.

"I'm gonna bet you everything I own that they will find everything they're looking for, if they conduct a full investigation. Nobody ever questioned my wife when she failed to demand an autopsy."

To suggest that anyone associated with James Brown was responsible for Darren's death would be nothing more than speculation - speculation that emerged in the press multiple times when Darren's death was made public.

It is clear to all that Darren Lumar was executed. The police are confident of this fact. The last of the five shots was intentionally directed toward his thumb - a specific message from the executioner. The list of suspects and potential enemies is so long, that drawing any conclusion would be without merit.

Domestic violence played a role in Yamma and Darren's separation. Yamma was charged with assault for cutting Darren with a butcher knife. Allegedly, Darren initiated the violence. That may have been the least of Darren's problems. Rumors of rape, infidelity, extensive fraud, theft, forgery, "creative financing" and ponzi schemes plagued Darren daily. The list of people willing and able to send a message was extensive.

Nevertheless, questions remain. Why did Yamma not ask for an autopsy?

She has remained silent on this question. Interestingly, the hospital where James Brown died was just a few minutes from her home in Atlanta.

Yamma was one of the first to be called by Charles Bobbit from the hospital. She spoke tenderly at the funeral:

"Thank you, Augusta. I'm going to be brief because my sister (Deanna) so graciously thanked everyone and I'm forever grateful for everybody's hard work and help in all of this. I just want to say, I lived in Atlanta and I didn't get to see him as much as I wanted to. But I got the first phone call to go see him in the hospital because they couldn't do anything until family came. It was kind of like my own little special thing that he was in Atlanta with me. I went to the hospital and sat with him for a long time before anybody ever came. And I just talked to him. And it was just special for me. I just want to say, thank you, Augusta. I was born here and I love Augusta. And although, like I said, I don't get a chance to come back here very often, but this is where daddy would want to be. And just want to say thank you to my husband for being my rock, and my beautiful children for loving their grandfather so much. Thank you, Augusta."

Until Yamma shares her story, we are left to wonder.

Several individuals have raised questions regarding the death of James Brown including his former publicist, Jacque Hollander. She said publicly, "It was an ordered hit." Hollander has said she has evidence to corroborate her claim. To date, that evidence has not been made public.

Say Goodbye

Al Sharpton took control. That is how he does things.

The Reverend is charismatic, exciting, and intoxicating. He is one of a kind. Buddy Dallas said, "Rev. Al Sharpton is without a doubt the finest contemporaneous speaker in the country. There is not a close second. His funeral service was magnificent. His memorial service was the most moving sermon I have ever heard."

Al Sharpton spoke. It was toward the end of the program. I was standing right behind him and he said something not quite true. The drive to the Apollo Theater was not correct. He began by graciously giving credit to the funeral home director Charlie Reid. It is true; the "caretaker" had worked tirelessly for several days for what must have been difficult arrangements (most mortals do not have three services in three separate states– tens of thousands of mourners - and the King of Pop return from self-imposed exile to attend the funeral). But, he should have mentioned William Murrell.

Sharpton continued, "When Deanna (James' sister), Yamma, Nicey, Larry, Terry and Daryl decided they wanted a 24 karat gold casket, I had never heard of it. But he (Charlie Reid) went and found it.

He said, 'Reverend, you got one problem.'
I said, 'What's that?'

He said, 'No small private plane can carry that weight. It's almost 500 pounds by itself. Then, with Mr. Brown, it's another 150 - 160 pounds.'

So I got to the funeral home that night and we arranged to put it on a Delta flight, but it left while we waited on the casket (Delta could not get insurance for the cargo).

So Mr. Reid said, 'I'll tell you what, he got to make it to the Apollo. And he never missed the Apollo. I'll drive the body all night.'

I said, "Well, I'll get in the car and ride with you. You ain't going to out James Brown me."

Again, Reverend Sharpton should have mentioned William Murrell. William was my father's personal driver for the last decade of his life. It was Murrell who drove the body 800 miles to the Apollo Theater in Harlem and who returned the Godfather and "The Rev." safely home the very next day.

One biographer stated the casket was solid gold. A 500 pound solid gold casket? C'mon man. Do the math.

***

William Murrell

When he died, I took his body to the Apollo Theater in New York City. It was with Rev. Al Sharpton, the funeral director, and my assistant driver. They muminized his body so he would never rot. I helped change his clothes twice. When we opened up the casket his body was drenched with

42

sweat. It was all wet. The chemicals had caused moisture to surround the body. So we had to change clothes.

By the time the undertaker had finished preparing the body, and the children ordered the casket, it was getting late. The liner in the casket did not match the outfit he had on, so the children sent the liner out to have another liner installed that would match his outfit inside the casket. By the time that was done it was too late to get a plane to New York. They called me.

It was the funeral home Director that called. He said, "Mr. Murrell, can you take Mr. Brown to New York?" What? I thought they were kidding. How could I possibly say no to the Godfather? I told them that I would do it. I called one of my drivers and we went straight to the funeral home. We took all the back seats out of my new Ford van. I left one row of seats for the undertaker and Rev. Al Sharpton.

We drove in six-hour shifts. Nonstop. We stayed with the body for 12 hours and then we turned right around and sped back toward South Carolina. We worked 36 hours in the two-day period so that we could get the body back to the next funeral in Augusta, Georgia. That was on a Thursday. We left New York City Thursday night and arrived in Augusta, Georgia at 8 AM the next morning. We had the body ready by 1 PM on Friday. They had the private funeral at Carpentersville Baptist Church in South

Carolina. That Saturday, we had the funeral at the James Brown Auditorium in Augusta.

It was the public funeral service on Saturday where Michael Jackson showed up. Michael came to Augusta on Friday night when we had the body at the funeral home. Michael did James Brown's hair. Michael Jackson is the one who put the curl in the front of James Brown's hair. He stayed with the body privately for one hour. Everybody had to leave the funeral home and Michael Jackson stayed with James Brown privately for one hour.

It was incredible seeing Michael Jackson for the first time. He did not look real. I'm serious. He's plastic, man. His whole face was a color that you have never seen before in your entire life. I'm serious.

Michael Jackson rented three vehicles from me: he rented three SUVs; two for security and one for him. He stayed at the Partridge Inn when he came to town.

He was fragile. The way that he carried himself - it looked to me as if he moved too quickly one way or the other, his body would break. I was really scared of him. I'm serious man. If you looked at him, he doesn't look real. He doesn't look real at all. He looked just like a Frankenstein. When you see him on TV, you do not get the real picture. You need to see him in person. It was scary. That was the first person that I ever met in my life that looked scary to me. I cannot be with him at night. It scared the daylights out of me.

Again I tell you, Michael Jackson is the one that put the curl in James Brown's hair. He felt him all over the body. Michael wanted to know why James Brown was so hard. When they muminized his body everything went hard.

Michael spoke at the funeral. He said, "James Brown is my greatest inspiration, I never saw a performer perform like James Brown. And right then and there, I knew that was what I wanted to do for the rest of my life, because of James Brown."

The casket was 24 karat gold-plated. It cost more than $30,000. All of his funeral expenses are still not paid for. I believe they're still in the hole about $17,000. I just got the rest of my money from the estate about a year ago - in 2013. Seven years after his death. They were $15,000 in the hole with me. This was for three months of ground transportation as well as taking his body to New York and back.

The trip that night was history. I was traveling 90 miles per hour trying to get to New York. Al Sharpton was just talking away. We all had conversations about the good times with James Brown.

It was so weird driving his body to New York and Mr. Brown was not able to say a word.

On the way to the Apollo Theater in Harlem, Rev. Sharpton talked about the good old times. Rev. Sharpton married one of James Brown's backup singers. James

45

Brown had bought Rev. Sharpton a house here in Augusta, Georgia. Rev. Sharpton used to live in South Carolina, not too far from James Brown house. He told stories about how James Brown had introduced him to his wife.

Rev. Sharpton used to travel with James Brown. He was a religious aid to Mr. Brown. He also did a lot of PR work for Mr. Brown. I have picked up Mr. Sharpton many times. I still pick him up when he comes to town. He comes here a lot. I picked him up when he preached at Springfield Baptist Church. Springfield Baptist Church is one of the oldest Baptist churches in the entire South. That is where Morehouse College started.

That trip was a nice trip. I actually helped the funeral director change the clothes. That was not easy. It was difficult when his body would move. We had to rearrange everything. It was a full open casket. It made it much easier to have a full open casket rather than those that only open at the top. When they showed his body they showed the whole thing.

The New York Daily News wrote an entire piece on my experience.

When we got the body to New York, we went to Rev. Al Sharpton's office. That is where we changed the clothes. We then moved the casket from my van to a hearse. We took it from the hearse to the horse and buggy. We then walked 40 blocks with the Godfather of Soul down Malcolm X Blvd. and then on 125th St. to the Apollo theater. It was like a parade. People were everywhere. We had a police escort.

We had a police escort from New Jersey to New York. Once we arrived in New Jersey, Rev. Al Sharpton had everything arranged for a police escort. They would meet us and escort us the last part of the journey. We were a haulin' buggy baby. Yes sir.

The way they drive in New York is really crazy. They were trying to get in between the police escort and the van. They were trying to cut in between us. I was so used to having James Brown led by a police escort that I got right on their tail.

***

Super Frank, of Intrigue Music took over the financial side of the funeral, Al Sharpton and the others spent the money. $53,000 was the charge for the hotel and a variety of funeral expenses. The funeral home was not paid for years. The casket alone was tens of thousands of dollars depending on who you believe. The lining had to be changed to match his three outfits. We needed to change to something neutral, we went with white.

We placed gloves on my father's hands. They were burnt from drug use. The public did not need to see how my father overcame the pain of his illness.

***

The Rev. was at his very best that day. Those that needed to be included were included. He handled every one of us with finesse. Reintroducing Michael after exile in Bahrain was a delicate matter. After spending hours with the body (some say it was one hour - others suggest five) he wanted to see the body one more time. He approached the coffin with Rev. Sharpton, Jessie Jackson, and members of the family. He was repeatedly drawn toward the casket. Finally, he kissed my father's forehead and was guided away.

During the services Michael said, "James Brown is my greatest inspiration. Ever since I was a small child, no more than six years old, my mother would wake me no matter what time it was, if I was sleeping, no matter what I was doing, to watch the television to see the master at work. And when I saw him move, I was mesmerized. I never saw a performer perform like James Brown. And right then and there, I knew that was what I wanted to do for the rest of my life, because of James Brown. James Brown, I shall miss you, and I love you so much and thank you for everything."

He had expressed similar sentiments during the Black Entertainment Television (BET) awards in 2003.

***

The makeup, the curl, the outfit was all James Brown. It wasn't just hard for Michael to say goodbye - it was hard for all those who loved the man. Danny Ray (the Cape Man and long-time friend), had a particularly difficult time.

48

Danny Ray said simply, "At his funeral, I put a cape over his coffin. Everybody broke down and cried."

That is all Danny really can say. He had introduced my father with unbelievable energy since the mid 1960s. They were close - as thick as thieves. The cape act was as much a part of the James Brown show as Sex Machine or Papa's Got a Brand New Bag. He began the funeral service, "Ladies and Gentlemen, it's Staaaaarrrr time!"

He welcomed everyone to the arena including Michael Jackson, MC Hammer and "many, many more celebrities."

What Danny didn't know, and what many who were in attendance didn't know, is we were now dead men walking. When the spirit of James Brown left this world - he took ours with him.

Danny would lose his home before the year ended. He battled crack cocaine and alcohol addiction. He was arrested and served time in jail. He, like my father in his younger years, had unresolved tax issues with the IRS. All of his assets have been seized. He now has a few photo albums and pictures on the wall to remind him, and anyone with the time to listen, of better days. He is able to pick up an occasional gig now and then - but leads a solitary existence living in a small corner apartment contained within a senior housing complex.

He is one of a kind.

If the producers of Get on Up can omit Danny Ray from the movie - they might as well have omitted James Brown. The two were inseparable.

The funeral was troubling for some. A long-time associate said:

"When I looked at the casket, he (James Brown) literally scared me. I jumped back. It wasn't him. I don't know if it was because they traveled with the body far too long. They traveled to New York, the Apollo Theater and back to Augusta, Georgia. You need to understand, Mr. Brown's legs were always bowed. In the casket he was like a porcelain doll. His legs were so straight. That was not the Mr. Brown I knew. He would walk around like a peacock; always strutting. His legs were always bowed. This was not the man I knew. When I saw him in the casket I started backing up, and I wasn't backing up slow. I couldn't believe it. I couldn't look at him anymore. It was very hard."

Some say Brown is coming back and snatching people from the grave. Miss Overton is gone. Judge Bradley is gone. Half the band is dead and others are quickly on their way out. Arthur Dixon is dead.

***

Al Sharpton said something very interesting during the funeral. Only a few on the inside had any idea what he was talking about. He said, "As they say, Andre White and Mr. Cannon, Mr. Dallas, all of them that stood with him, we got to keep the family together! Sidney Miller, we got to keep it together, because Mr. Brown's legacy is important."

"We got to keep the family together" lasted until the benediction offered by Jessie Jackson. We all knew what Sharpton was talking about – the will, the trust, and the legacy of James Brown. However, the children, Sharpton, Cannon, Dallas, Tomi Rae and others who remain alive, are now deeply divided.

Buddy Dallas remembers the event matter-of-factly. "Rev. Sharpton asked me about the will after the funeral of Mr. Brown. He asked me if he was included. I told him that he was not. We have not had the occasion to speak since that time."

David Cannon has similar memories, "We ate together sitting at the table after the funeral. We had dinner together that night at the hotel after the funeral. We sat with the editor of Rolling Stone, MC Hammer, and Al Sharpton. He was sitting right next to me."

When Cannon talked to the children before my father's death, everyone wanted to know what piece of the pie was for them. Even Rev. Sharpton wanted to know. He was informed that he was not included in the will. Sharpton then turned into an advocate for Deana and the other children in order to receive an inheritance.

My father wanted to be buried right between his wife Adrienne and his father Joe Brown. He said, "If we can't be a family in life, we can be family in death." His body has been preserved and the remains are located in a crypt on (my sister) Deanna Brown's property.

Finally, I wanted to keep the band together after my father died. We spent more time with each other than we did with our own families. My father told me how to do it. Unfortunately, it was like a spell came over the band. We broke up immediately after he died. Some of us have kept in touch after we broke up, but it was a big financial blow for all of us when my father died. None of us had learned how to manage money, because James just handed out cash. Many in the band (that are still alive) now live in poverty.

From Adrienne to Tomi Rae

'She was the Devil if the Devil ever walked the earth.'

That is the most common response when asked about Adrienne Brown. She was evil - beautifully evil.

My father attracted troubled women like darkness attracts devils. He was a magnet for wayward souls. He may have had an intuitive connection with their tormented past. My father liked to play with fire. Is anyone surprised he got burned? James Brown was, after all, Mr. Dynamite.

Like attracts like.

I watched my father beat the shit out of his wife when I was 16. I walked out of the house and slammed the door. I headed straight for the airport - I had no idea how I was going to pay for a ticket home. He drove up a few minutes later. "Son, get in the car now. It ain't going to be like that." I was so angry I wanted to beat him. We both had terrible tempers.

Like attracts like.

Having matured just a little over the years and walked my own bumpy road, I am left to ask: Why did so many around my father hate Adrienne and Tomi Rae? Were they jealous knowing these two women were going to take their piece of his pie? My father invited them to his party. He hunted them down. They would have been fools for declining an invitation to dine with the Godfather.

Like attracts like.

53

My father divorced Velma in 1969 and married Deedee in 1970. His divorce from Deidre Jenkins was finalized in 1981 and he met Adrienne Lois Rodriguez in 1982. Adrienne died in 1996 and he rescued Tomi Rae the very next year. My father was famous for saying, "I'm single and I like to mingle." He liked to mingle a whole lot. He hated being single.

My father loved Adrienne. I can't explain it. Maybe Al Sharpton can – he was the one who brought them together after my dad spotted her while performing on Solid Gold. When he performed, I Got You (I Feel Good) he must have been singing to Adrienne. She was multiracial and stunning. Would it surprise anyone to know she was abandoned as a little girl, raised in foster care, and then settled with a relative on the bad side of town?

Rev. Sharpton said that Adrienne was called a 'nigger lover' by people in the community. I wish I would have asked him who had used that word. It was no surprise to me that Rev. Al felt my father's arrest in 1988 had racial overtones. He was determined to make the point. Few listened. Tragically, Tomi Rae encountered the same racism from the police in South Carolina.

Adrienne was James Brown's "Wooga." She was also the one who screamed, "You black-assed nigger" when they fought. They loved hard and they fought hard. Adrienne was not the only woman that called my father a "nigger." "Black-assed" was mild compared to words I

54

heard during other fights. Twisted and hurtful racial slurs hurt my father and left him feeling dejected. However, I was with him on more than one occasion when he gave back just as much as he got. "Nigger" just pissed him off.

I tolerated Adrienne. Sometimes I liked her, sometimes I didn't. My mother, Bea Ford got along with her just fine. My mother was not going to get bent out of shape because of Adrienne. She knew James Brown better than anyone.

My father called my mother and asked her if he should get married again. She said, "Hell no!" She told him not to do it. This was before he met Adrienne. She told him he could have any woman that he wanted in the world. They would talk like that. They were good friends. My father had a laugh. There was really no reason for him to get married. He was the player of all players. He had plenty of money. He got tired of his women quick.

Adrienne loved PCP every bit as much as she loved my father. PCP killed her. Many people say her drug use far exceeded his. My father would not eat anything she prepared for him. He feared her cooking would be laced with PCP or some other drug. She had a habit of "cooking" with various herbs and oils.

Adrienne's love/hate relationship with my father was explained as an expression of drugs mingled with Roots magic, Voodoo Hoodoo, whatever spell she could cast. More than a few people found her passed out laying butt up naked on the floor of their home. That was not a pretty sight.

Adrienne ran head first into law enforcement more than my father. Dad's lawyers had her drug supplier "popped" at the airport. Adrienne was in the wrong place at the wrong time. This what the AP reported on May 20, 1988:

"Mrs. Brown, 38, of Beech Island, S.C., was arrested at the airport in nearby Augusta on Friday afternoon after arriving on a flight from New York. Police acted on a tip that she would be carrying drugs, said Ron Maher of the Augusta Police vice and narcotics unit.

She was taken to the Richmond County-Augusta Law Enforcement Center, where police said a search turned up a further two vials suspected to contain PCP hidden in her blouse.

On April, 9 and on May 10, Mrs. Brown was also arrested for possession of PCP. She maintained that she was set up."

That is a portion of the story from the AP. They covered "the facts" well. Please pay attention to the line, "Police acted on a tip that she would be carrying drugs…" Who could have possibly tipped them off? Of course it was my father's inner-circle. They needed a hot performer – not a performer that was hot on PCP. They cared deeply for my father. We were all invested in the success of James Brown, even if it meant his wife would serve time.

Adrienne, or Alphie as she was called by others, was arrested on September 3, 1987 for driving under the influence, possession of a controlled substance, failing to stop for a blue light and criminal trespass. The story is now infamous.

U.S. Representative Douglas Barnard of Georgia delivered a flowery political speech hoping to land votes and campaign contributions. He enthusiastically stated "James is indeed our No. 1 ambassador!" Adrienne's lawyer, Allen W. Johnson, pathetically argued that as the spouse of "America's No. 1 ambassador" she would legally fall under the protection of the diplomatic immunity umbrella. I can't believe he wasn't disbarred for that defense. He quickly withdrew as he so insightfully "determined that the congressman intended his comments as a goodwill gesture and a figure of speech." Really?

The number of charges, arrests, and investigations involving James and Adrienne Brown during this time was tiring for the police – they said so themselves. The number of arrests could not be counted on both hands and feet. What will never be known is how many arrests Buddy Dallas kept from ever taking place? To know Buddy is to love him. I suspect the police had Dallas on speed dial.

Adrienne died following a liposuction procedure in Beverly Hills. She had not been in contact with my father for several days and then quickly demanded he send a $60,000+ wire to the doctor. She used the same physician as Joan Rivers. According to my father's staff, she had 35 pounds of material removed during a single procedure. They believe the legal limit in California at the time was seven pounds.

The "recovery center" was little more than a high class hotel room - this type of work would never have been completed in a licensed facility. When you combine Valium, Vicodin, Demerol, morphine, and PCP as an elixir to relieve pain, death is a probability more than a possibility.

My father refused to take legal action. He said, "It would be blood money." James Brown would be at the end of a long and distinguished line of Hollywood celebrities already wanting their pound of flesh.

Keith Graham, my father's security detail, may have known Adrienne best. Unlike others, Adrienne posed no threat to Keith.

"When I joined Mr. Brown after his incarceration, it took me many years to fully understand what was going on in his life. I was surprised by that. There was so much going on with his management team, with the office, there was so much crap. All he expected anyone to do was their job. All Mr. Brown wanted was his money and to be able to enjoy performing.

With all the shit he was going through with his wife Adrienne, the drugs he was using and some of the people around him, it was terrible. How he made it through is amazing to me.

Adrienne Brown was a very smart character. Mrs. James Brown! She was the Godmother. She was a very smart character. People took her for granted. I spent a lot of time with Mrs. Brown. Believe me, she was not a fool. She knew exactly what she was doing and exactly how she was doing it. She knew why she was doing it. Many people sold Adrienne short because she played a role. Let me tell you, they got it wrong. She essentially took her own life; she would not listen to anybody.

She loved James Brown with every fiber of her being. They were like peas and carrots. It was a love-hate relationship. You know how you can love somebody to death, literally? Their relationship was unexplainable. Mr. Brown could not even explain it to me. I would ask him, "What is it with the two of you?" He didn't know how to answer the question. That was all I needed to know. If he couldn't answer the question there simply was no answer. They would fight like cats and dogs, but they loved each other. They loved each other so hard - but it was weird.

They were good together. They were A and B. Adrienne was 'A' and Mr. Brown was 'B'. Adrienne was very much an "A" type personality. I know she called him terrible names, but that is how they loved each other. Yes, she called him the worst names imaginable. If you read it, it is shocking. It was just how they lived their lives. You had

to see the War of the Roses and then witness what
happened the very next day. You had to watch the chairs
fly one day, and see them kiss the next. It was that kind of
relationship.

Adrienne was a bitch. She was the nastiest character.
If she was still alive you could've had a reality show that
would've made you millions. There was not a good bone in
that woman's body. I found the good - but it took me quite
a while. I could not break through the exterior she had. She
was an incredible individual. It destroyed Mr. Brown when
she went away.

Even with all of their violent history together, they had
each other's back. They were tight. Even though they were
fighting, feuding, kicking the shit out of each other, and
shooting at each other at times, that is just the way they
were. There was nothing negative you could say about
Adrienne to James Brown. There is nothing negative you
could say to Adrienne about James Brown. They would kill
you. They may kill each other separately, but they had each
other's back. If you came up against them together you
might as well leave the room. You don't want Adrienne
pissed at you - she would tear you apart. You would
quickly find that you had attacked the wrong person.

Adrienne was the top whore – all the others fell under
her. She happens to be "The Madame." She accepted that
sexual lifestyle. There were times when it pushed her over
the edge. She would go into a tirade. Her anger actually

made James Brown feel good; it was an indication she actually cared. It made him smile. In some way her rage was a reflection of her love for him. That is ridiculous. That is no way to live. But that was her choice. He messed around on her and she knew it. It was like a circus.

***

David Cannon has a different story to tell.

The police did arrest Adrienne once on a different occasion. She was at the Augusta airport. She was caught with PCP. I didn't even know about it until it was all over. Buddy Dallas got her out of trouble. She had someone out of New York bring her drugs. She was sending this particular girl a lot of money. The police found out about it and had the young woman arrested. Adrienne was in the wrong place at the wrong time. She went to the airport when the woman landed. They were both arrested and taken to jail. That is where Buddy Dallas stepped in.

Oh my Lord, (Mr. Brown) called me more than one time in the middle of the night, particularly when he was fighting with Adrienne. One night he called at 3 o'clock in the morning. I heard her hollering at him and banging on the bedroom door. She was going to kill him. She shot through the door with a pistol. He said to me, "Mr. Cannon, I just want you to stay on the phone with me. If you don't want to talk that's fine. I just need you to stay on the phone with me." And I did.

61

He would call my wife and talk to her about Adrienne. In my opinion, if the Devil ever walked on this earth, it was in the form of that woman. That was her. Then with his last woman, his so-called wife, Tomi Rae, he would call my wife and asked her to take Tomi Rae out shopping. He wanted her to go buy things. He wanted Tomi Rae to be around my wife more, so she could learn to act like a lady. That was the kind of relationship my wife and I had with the man.

The sad thing about it, was he really did love Adrienne. He really loved her. It was sad that he lost her. It was sad that he had to put up with all of her shenanigans.

There was a time when we were traveling to Atlanta. I believe we were going to talk to the Coca-Cola people. I drove my car to his home to pick him up. Naturally, we were taking a limousine to Atlanta and the car was going to take both of us to Atlanta.

Adrienne wanted to go. She was high on drugs. I think she was also into witchcraft. She was into roots. She was into witch doctors. At this time, however, she could hardly walk due to her drug use. He told her that she could not go. She yelled - yes, she was going to go. When we left she was on her knees in the foyer of the house.

We walked out and arrived in Atlanta around 8:00 PM or 9:00 PM. that night. The next morning I turned on the news to see that spouse abuse charges had been filed. It was reported that Brown had beaten his wife. It was all over the news that he had beat his wife the night before. That could not have been. He was with me. The truth is, she fell down because she was so full of drugs. She bumped her head and told the police that Mr. Brown had beat her.

I immediately called the sheriff. I knew the sheriff. The sheriff told me that the police were looking for Mr. Brown. I said, "I know where he is. He is right here in Atlanta with me. We came over together yesterday. He could not have beaten her last night, he was with me."

That part of the story never got on the news. The news simply reported that they were looking for Mr. Brown for domestic violence charges. They never came back on the air and retracted their story. They never admitted their mistake. She would hurt herself to get back at him. She would steal his money.

There was a reason why he would not keep as much cash as he was accustomed to at the house. I'm not going to tell you where he kept it hidden. Well, if the truth be told, he had $90,000 in the suspended ceiling of the pool house. She found it and she took it. She was always looking for his money. Naturally, she spent a lot of the money on drugs. But her mother was also in California. She gave a lot of money to her. And there were others that she was giving money to. Mr. Brown gave a lot of money to her family and many others in California.

Adrienne had him convinced that she worked for the government, and that she had special powers. He went to the dentist to have some fillings put in his teeth. There was a radio antenna about 2 miles from the house. She had him convinced that the government was listening to everything he said through the fillings in his teeth.

I never saw her with any roots or any drugs in her hand, but I was told that she had a lot of involvement in witchcraft. While I didn't see it personally - I did see the results of it.

Mr. Brown told me several times that she put drugs in his food. That is why he would not eat anything prepared at the house when she was home. She would put PCP in his food. He would not eat anything cooked or prepared at the house because he didn't know what she had put in it.

He kept her around because he loved her. He absolutely loved her. I have been with them when he was talking about her and had tears running down his cheeks. I don't know exactly why he loved her. I have thought about that a number of times.

When she was young, and he first met her, she was a very attractive woman. She was the kind of woman who would go to the bank in a bed gown and house slippers. I think she was on drugs when she did that. Over the years she became overweight. That is why she died in California.

She would talk to me many times and say, "Mr. Cannon, you are handling all the money. This is what I need." I would say, "Mrs. Brown, you are going to have to talk to Mr. Brown. I cannot do what you're asking."

She would get mad at me. She knew I would not let it go unless Mr. Brown gave the order.

I don't know how much money Adrienne Brown spent over time. I do know that I gave her $1 million in 1992. It was at one time. I don't know how she spent the money. I know that she was supporting her brother and her mother out in Los Angeles. I don't know what she did with her money, and at that time I didn't want to know what she was doing with her money.

When we settled with the IRS, the government requested that we re-file tax returns for Adrienne Brown. She and Mr. Brown had never filed together. I told them, "Absolutely not!" We were not going to do that. That could not be part of the deal or the deal was off.

I turned to Mr. Brown and looked him right in the eye. I said, "Are you ready to go now?" He was. The IRS stopped us and asked that we let them discuss the matter privately. They returned after 20 minutes. They informed us that they would take that provision off the table.

I had many interactions with Adrienne Brown over the years. Unfortunately, when she passed, I had absolutely no reaction at all. I was surprised by that. That was odd for me. When you're around somebody, you will usually have a reaction to their loss. I was caught off guard when I had no reaction at all. That has never happened to me before.

Adrienne Brown had way too much plastic surgery done at one time. It was a violation of medical practices.

The toxicology report came back and said she was full of PCP. The doctors provided for her the proper pain medications after the procedure. That was not good enough for Adrienne. She had drugs brought into her room. It was the combination of the two that ultimately killed her.

Buddy Dallas has told this story on many occasions.

There was something inside Mr. Brown that kept him from the greatness he could've achieved. It was as if he couldn't believe the incredible success he had enjoyed. He would allow something like a marital problem with Adrienne to stand in the way of success. She had significant - significant - drug abuse problems. She really hated Mr. Brown. It was a love-hate relationship. I have heard her say, repeatedly, "I am going to bring that Nigger to his knees if that is the last thing I do!"

She would get all worked up on drugs. Mr. Brown would call in the middle of the night. She was so extremely jealous. She was infested with this strong desire to hurt him. She could infuriate Mr. Brown like no one else.

Adrienne Brown was a kleptomaniac to the point that the private company who provided the jet for Mr. Brown had to stop using silver. They had to start using plastic. If it was silver, she was going to take it out of the plane. If it was shiny she was going to take it with her.

I'll never forget when we were on a particular trip. As we were going through baggage clearance I reached down, as a gentleman, to help her with her bag. Mr. Brown was infuriated with what I was doing. I was just trying to be a gentleman. He said to me, "Mr. Dallas, put that bag down. Now!" He pulled me to the side and said, "Mr. Dallas, that bag will put you in jail." It must have weighed fifty pounds. I never asked what was in the bag.

I did not realize what I was doing. I was just trying to be a gentleman. However, once Mr. Brown set the boundaries you did not dishonor him. I never touched her bag after that.

There were certain restaurants that barred her from entrance. They would not take her back in.

Mr. Brown only harms himself. He never harmed another person. If you ask about Adrienne, his wife, please remember that she was so out of her head on drugs. You could not believe a word she said. She stole from him. She made false reports to the police. She made false 911 calls. She called Mr. Brown the "N-word." That was her word. She said that to me many times.

I would tell his wife, "Mrs. Brown, if you make that report, what is going to happen to you?" She never answered that question.

Adrienne Brown was a real addict. She hated Mr. Brown. Whatever propensity Mr. Brown had, she exacerbated all of the problems. She would take cookies into the prison - they were laced with drugs. I believe she convinced herself that Mr. Brown was far worse of a man than he really was. I know she falsified reports against him.

Adrienne is buried next to my grandfather, Pops. This is what is written on her grave:

ADRIENNE LOIS BROWN
MARCH 9, 1950
JANUARY 6, 1996
SHE WAS A NATIVE OF LOS ANGELES
CALIFORNIA AND THE WIFE OF THE GODFATHER
OF SOUL, JAMES BROWN.
SHE WAS A DEDICATED FIGHTER FOR HUMANITY,
A LOVER OF ALL PEOPLE, A PERSON WHO WAS
NOT GIVEN THE WORLD ON A SILVER PLATTER
BUT ONE WHO HAD TO WORK VERY LONG AND
HARD FOR EVERYTHING SHE ACCOMPLISHED IN
LIFE.
SHE WAS A DILIGENT PARTNER, A LADY, A
LOVER AND FRIEND.
BECAUSE OF THE LOVE AND AFFECTION SHE HAD
FOR HER FATHER-IN-LAW JOSEPH "POP" BROWN,
SHE REQUESTED TO BE BURIED NEXT TO HIM
HERE IN AUGUSTA, TO BE JOINED BY HER
HUSBAND JAMES BROWN AND EVERYONE IN HIS
FAMILY.
I WILL ALWAYS HAVE EVERLASTING LOVE FOR
YOU AND I WILL NEVER FORGET YOU. KNOW
ONE DAY WE WILL MEET EACH OTHER

AGAIN…ME, YOU,"POP" AND ALL OF OUR
FAMILY.
WE'LL BE TOGETHER AGAIN FOREVER. WITH
TEARS IN MY EYES AND PAIN IN MY HEART, I SAY
SO LONG…

YOUR "WOOGAR"
JAMES
I LOVE YOU, SUGAR!!!

People write the damndest things on gravestones.

***

The story of Tomi Rae is tragic on so many levels.
Vicki Anderson spent some time with my father the last
week of his life. Vicki was a life-long friend of the family.
She and Bobby Byrd (founder of the Famous Flames) made
a beautiful couple. Her story, along with Keith Graham,
provides a transition from Adrienne to Tomi Rae.

<u>Vicki Anderson</u> – Wife of Bobby Byrd

James Brown has done some nice things for me. He
introduced me to the world in the Mike Douglas show in
1970. He has also done some terrible things because of
Bobby. That was because I chose Bobby over James.
Bobby Byrd was such an honorable man.

Women need to understand that James Brown knew
that I couldn't be his wife. If a man beats all of his women,

what makes you think he is not going to beat you? That doesn't make sense. He was that type of a person. He never had a woman, that he called his woman, whom he didn't kick or stomp. What could possibly have led me to think that he wouldn't do the same thing to me?

We were friends to his death because I said 'No.' He really respected me for that. If you look at the biography – the only singer you are going to see a picture of in that book is Vicki Anderson. His wife, Adrienne, also known as Alphie, was in the book, but I was the only singer.

Adrienne Brown was not the kind of person that you could say nice things about. Brown did her like he did all of the rest of his women. You need to treat them good. You can't get blood out of a turnip.

I thought James was too old to make the baby with Tomi Rae. Tomi Rae was good to James and good for James. The estate did her wrong. I was in the car with James, Bobby, and Bobbit the last week of his life and Mr. Brown said he was going to give Tomi Rae 17.5 %. I know that is true.

***

<u>Keith Graham</u> -- Bodyguard

Tomi Rae saved Mr. Brown. We would not have had him as long as we did if it wasn't for her. She brought new life into his soul. He was going downhill fast after the loss of Adrienne. He was going down a deep dark path. Tomi gave him hope. He needed another Adrienne in his life.

70

Tomi Rae does not even have one ounce of what Adrienne had in her. Adrienne was Satan, Tomi Rae was a harmless little she devil. Tomi Rae jumped into the James Brown experience and it was way over her head. She was a good girl in some ways. We spent some time together.

Nobody could replace Adrienne. Tomi Rae tried. She tried the best she could. She put up with a lot of crap. That is what the lifestyle of being a celebrity is all about. She wanted to go for the ride and unfortunately that is what she got. She can't be upset; she could have left any time.

She did not know how to keep Mr. Brown. I told her how to keep him.

When you talk about James Brown you have to understand that there is both good and bad. The irony is I think he actually enjoyed both.

Adrienne was just the top whore, relative to all of the other whores he was banging. He did the same thing to Tomi Rae. He made her the top Madame. The problem was - she was never the top. Nobody loved her. Nobody respected her. Nobody cared about her as a human being.

You need to understand James Brown banged everybody in the band. He banged everybody around the band. That is why everybody around him thought they were so special. Why would she be brought in to the circle? She was the white girl brought in, and many around the band were angry because they had spent decades with Mr. Brown. They were jealous. They were pissed off. They wanted to be "the one" for Mr. Brown. Each person was temporarily "the one" - but for little more than moments. When they were no longer "the one" on top - they became jealous.

Tomi Rae was brought into the life of the Godfather because he was hurting. She was the flavor-of-the-day and it took hold. The women around James Brown were livid. She embraced an attitude and arrogance about being the new Mrs. James Brown and that didn't work for anyone. That did not work out well. She couldn't carry herself like Adrienne. She wasn't refined. Mr. Brown did not give Tomi Rae the same status as he did to Adrienne.

***

Tomi Rae was gracious enough to provide an extensive story for this book. It would be fair to say that I have not always been her biggest fan. I, like many others, was suspicious of her motives.

After my father died and I witnessed how Tomi Rae was treated, I told certain people that they needed to "back off." Whatever you believe about Little Man (James Brown II) my father gave that child his name. My father's name is on the birth certificate. If DNA evidence proves to the contrary then so be it. Please be clear - my father loved that child in such a way that I was envious. My father was never that good to me as a little boy.

As for Tomi Rae, she was my father's problem, not mine. We still disagree on many things. We both have had battles with drug addiction. We both know where "bodies" are buried. There are some things that should be kept between husband and wife.

This is her story.

***

Tomi Rae

There are people that have taken advantage of me and my child. I want the truth to come out.

I am writing a book for young people, particularly artists and women, to help them understand that they can go from the "Outhouse to the White House." I don't want to see them make the same mistakes I have.

My husband was a wonderful man. Of course he had his demons. What people don't understand about my husband is that his demons are the consequence of the betrayal by those around him. Terrible things were done to him that were no fault of his own. He experienced racism in large measure. He had to be a "hard" man simply to protect himself. Many contributed to his pain - particularly those that surrounded him and asked him to work hard so they could become wealthy.

I never saw him beat a woman. That was not the man I knew. He had rules. He was a strict man. James Brown was a compassionate man. He was a good man regardless of what others might say.

James Brown's reputation regarding his sexual behavior was well-known when I met him. I had been an entertainer my whole life. I have been in a musical group since I was 11 years old. I understand the lifestyle, I get it. I understand the energy that a man like James Brown has. However, he was always "faithful" to me: My husband came home to me.

I was aware of his behavior relative to other women. I was not surprised by any of the other relationships he had. I excuse my husband for a lot of things because he was good to me. During our marriage he was not with women all over the world. He did have a couple of ladies in his life he had known for many years. They would help him in a variety of ways including taking care of him when he was sick. He had cancer and diabetes.

As far as the additional details of his sexual desire and behavior, I didn't want to know about it. I didn't want to hear about it. I would not ask him about it. He was a good man to me and for me. I do not consider James Brown having issues of infidelity. He always gave me the ultimate respect. When we were in the presence of a woman he previously had a relationship with, he made certain they were respectful. I was his wife.

It was a relationship many people might not understand. I don't care if they understand our relationship. The man had so much energy, the energy of the freight train. For me, I had to be mature about his needs and about our relationship. I consider that relationship as a very private matter.

I didn't want to change James Brown. I wanted to spend the rest of my life with him. James Brown was the Godfather of Soul! I entered that relationship with my eyes open. He was very clear with everyone that I was his wife.

When James Brown passed away, the people around him no longer had to respect me. They came after me with a vengeance.

Once I was pulled over by the South Carolina police. They told me I should be ashamed of myself. They told me that there are a lot of places where people can get "lost" in South Carolina. I challenged the officer and told him that was an unacceptable threat on my life. They said that it wasn't a threat. They said they were just trying to "warn me" that there are a lot of places that people can get lost or go missing in South Carolina. That is why, after James died, I grabbed my son and left. They did not like a white woman having a child with a black man.

I met James Brown through one of his background singers; Candice Hurst. We were in a band together for many years in Hollywood. She called me out of the blue. We had not seen each other for more than ten years. She said she wanted to pay me back for the time we had together and asked me to audition for James Brown. Who wouldn't want to sing with the Godfather of Soul, James Brown? I told her that she didn't owe me anything - she had nothing to pay back.

I met James Brown at the Hilton Hotel in Las Vegas. I went upstairs and I sang "Mercedes Benz" for my audition. He said that I was not a background singer. I really never left his side from that moment. He asked me if I would work on his songs and perform with him in San Francisco the very next day. I was performing as Janis Joplin in Las Vegas at that time. I told him I was interested. He asked me how long it would take to get ready. I told him I needed an hour. I packed a bag and I never left his side. This took place around 1997.

In 1998 I began living with him, but I still kept my place in Las Vegas. We had a son together. We were later married. I pretty much stayed by his side since the day we met. I was illegally married to man who deceived me. The court ruled that the marriage was "void ab initio" which means it was treated as invalid from the start. This ruling validates my marriage to James Brown in 2001 as legal and lawful.

Keith Graham, James Brown's security detail was great. He was there all the time. He took good care of James; he took good care of us.

James Brown was a fighter. He was a survivor. He needed someone by his side. He listened to my advice. He respected my perspective. So many of the people around him were "yes" men. I would not do that to him. I told him how I felt about many things. We had a mutual respect for each other; we were honest with each other.

James Brown was a real strong man.

Everybody said "yes" to my husband. These were the men of his business and legal entourage. They were with him before I got there. It was interesting; the people that said they loved him the most were also the people that said "yes" to him the most. "Yes Sir Mr. Brown!" If my husband said the sky was red - they would say the blue sky was red. It would frustrate me. That is the way they treated him. It made him feel bad. He didn't have anyone that he could trust.

I remember several times when he would say something, just to see if people would agree with him. He would respond back to them, "You ain't nothing." He was testing them to see if they were being real. It hurt his feelings that not everybody was straight.

He expressed to me privately that there were people around him he could not trust. He would often say, "Keep your friends close but keep your enemies closer." He then told me not to get involved and stay out of his problems. I would often voice my opinion when I thought people were doing him wrong. He would then tell me to stay out of it. He tried to protect me from the problems he had in his business. He told me I didn't understand what he was trying to do. I honored his request. I listened to the conversations and I watched what was being said. It was no longer my job to criticize.

I had to honor the roles and boundaries that we had for each other. I knew what he was when I married him. We had fights and arguments, but it wasn't like people think. I think many relationships would last longer if people understood their proper role within that relationship. Many people live in a fantasy. I tried to live in reality the best I could. He was the Godfather of Soul, James Brown. I did not come into the relationship thinking I could change him (his sexual behavior) or change his world. He had been in control for so long. I was there to support him and keep him around as long as I could. I thought the world was a better place with him.

Regarding my husband's drug use, he said, "Baby, you can tell everyone that I smoke, I smoke, I smoke." That is what he said. The reason why he would smoke was that it relaxed him and allowed him to see other's behavior more clearly. I don't understand it - but it was true. It put him into a different level, mentally and emotionally, where he could understand their motivations. If you talk to anybody that really knew Mr. Brown they will tell you that he really did know what was going on around him. He also knew how the future would play out.

He would contemplate everything. He was very thoughtful. He was very private. He didn't like to have outsiders around him until we actually went in public. He enjoyed being at home and listening to his music. He was always thinking, thinking, and thinking. He would smoke and then he would call up somebody and let them know, "I know what you are doing." He would take time to reflect and smoke and think about all that was going on around him.

I am primarily talking about PCP. There was really only a short period of time when we were together that he was doing that drug. There were people who would come around him when we were in New York and provide him drugs. Keith Graham was really good about keeping "that guy" (the drug dealer), away. A couple of times the man would get through security and then the drugs would get into him. It wasn't all the time. He really liked to smoke marijuana. That is what we are talking about mostly. He liked to put the marijuana in the cigarettes so it was not as harsh. He wanted the filter on the marijuana cigarette. PCP only came in a few times and when it did, it was a radical change in his personality.

At the end of his life there was another drug introduced. It was because of the cancer. I fought with him a lot about that drug. I thought that drug would kill them. I think that is the reason he is not here today. I believe that somebody gave him bad drugs while I was away for 30 days. I think it poisoned him. Somebody should have been there to take care of him.

When I was with him throughout our entire marriage, I would rub his legs between four and six hours a day. I had to. There were times when he could not get on stage and dance. I would rub his legs for three hours and then he could get up on stage and dance for two hours. I would rub them until he could go to sleep because he was in so much pain.

There were people who were supposed to be taking care of him that last month of his life while I was gone. Candice was one of them. They were supposed to make sure he was taking his medicine and eating the correct foods. They should have been rubbing down his legs and making sure he wasn't taking the bad drugs. These are things that anger me. All of these people that say they care so much about him, why were they not there? They all saw him in this condition. Why didn't somebody call me and let me know how he was? James would never admit to me that anything was wrong. When I left he was fine. When I would talk to him on the phone he would say, "I can't wait for you to come home." We would talk about the show we had coming up BB Kings.

He told me that I needed to get myself relaxed, that I needed to get myself better. He didn't tell me there was anything wrong with him. It was a total surprise to me when they called me and told me he had passed away. I was just getting ready to come home on a flight.

Mr. Washington, the caretaker of our house, worked hand in hand with me to make sure that drugs did not come into our house. Mr. Washington looked out for Mr. Brown. I believe the 30 days I was gone had a cumulative effect of all of the drugs he was taking. I feel guilty for leaving him prior to his death. I feel terrible because I needed to take care of me. I never would have gone if I didn't think there were people to take care of. It kills me to think that if I was there, I may have been able to save his life. I had to leave in order to save myself. He understood that.

Nobody wants to be around somebody that is telling them what to do all day. He would order everybody around. Nobody would want to be around someone with that kind of temperament. However, if you really love the man, it doesn't matter. You stand up to tell him to throw the drugs away. They should have done whatever it took to keep him alive. They should not have been angry with him because they were not being treated fairly.

I needed to leave the house because my father had passed away. I was taking several prescription drugs including Xanax, pain killers, and sleeping pills. The doctors had me on multiple drugs. I was on the road all the time. I was not able to get off of the drugs by myself. I told my husband that I needed to take the 30 days before the show on New Year's Eve to get clean.

We had just returned home from his huge tour in Europe. We had a very busy year in 2006. I wasn't allowed to take vacation at all. I was given one week off every six months. I actually got in a huge fight with him regarding my health. We paid $30,000 for me to enter treatment. It was a mountain retreat. I got off all of the medications.

Everybody at home was telling me my husband was fine. Candice Hurst told me that Mr. Brown was fine. Later, I found out Candice was doing more than "taking care of him." I believe the people around him, while I was gone, provided an environment where he could hurt himself. That is something that I would not do – and that is why we fought so much.

Gloria Daniels and Candice Hurst were two women that were with him the last week of his life. I had the final approval of women that were allowed to be with my husband.

Candice was around my husband because she did his hair while he was on the road. She was his hairdresser. She took care of his makeup. She helped him with many things. I was his hairdresser off and on. If I was too tired, Candice would help me. She would do his hair before and after the shows. Sometimes it was so exhausting taking care of the man. It was not an easy task. I needed somebody to help me. Candice was very helpful to us. She was supposed to be taking care of him for 30 days.

Gloria Daniels is somebody that I did not want around. I didn't like her. Every time I went on vacation, her name would come up. I knew she had been around for years and had been intimate with him. I learned, after returning home, that Gloria Daniels was with him for some of the time I was gone. I did not know before I left that she was coming over.

I was not happy about that. I never approved of Gloria, but I had no choice.

Whenever I went away - that is the woman who occupied his space. Now I understand why. Gloria was somebody who did a lot of drugs. That was the primary connection they had. They liked to do drugs together.

There was video footage that was intended to be used against me in court. As it turns out, the woman on tape was Gloria Daniels. The video footage was intended to prove I was unfaithful. That was not the case.

Gloria was with him and Candice was with him. I surmised that they were doing drugs while I was gone, and that is what killed him. That is what I think - although it is speculation on my part.

Candice feels very guilty about it until this day. She was the one that was with him the night before he died. She smoked crack with him the night before he died. If she did drugs with him the night before he died, what did she do with him prior?

Candice was not there when Gloria Daniels was there. Gloria Daniels would come around just for a couple of days at a time to get as much money as she could. Then she would leave. Gloria was more of a "party buddy" to him. She would not stick around. She was paid for her services. That description is just being kind.

Ms. Johnson was the other woman in his life that preceded me by decades. Ms. Johnson was class. Gloria was nothing more than a hooker from Atlanta. Ms. Johnson had known him for years. She cared for him and did not put up with his bullshit. I liked her. She died mysteriously as well.

I knew James' mother, Susie, was involved with Roots magic. My husband would tell me that Roots magic, voodoo-hoodoo, and witchcraft was real. He told me not to get involved with that kind of stuff. I was informed that I had a "root" on me. It is a form of a curse. I had no idea what he was talking about. I did not understand. Ms. Overton, our housekeeper, was the person who told him someone had put a "root" on me. It was so strange. I had crazy car accidents and other crazy things happening at that point. Later, Ms. Overton told me that the "root" had been taken off me.

Yes, there was some of that "Roots" magic going on. That is what happens in the rural part of South Carolina and Georgia. It is "old school" magic. It is frightening. I believe in Jesus Christ. I have raised my child to believe in the Lord. James also believed in the Lord.

We went to church almost every Sunday. We didn't miss a Sunday church service or a Sunday chicken dinner on our way home. That is what we did.

However, he knew it was a fine line. He told me to stay away from the darkness. He told me to stay out of it. He, and one of his close friends, knew a great deal about those practices. Whatever they did together, regarding this form of worship, was done in private. I don't know what it was.

What I do know is that my husband was a God fearing man. He was no devil worshiper. These are cultural ideas in the South. It would not be viewed as devil worshiping. It is something else entirely. I'm not accusing anyone of anything, but for me, there is only light and dark.

Mr. Brown and I would often take the private plane home to attend church services on Sunday. That is absolutely true. We went to church every Sunday possible, and James Brown knew every song. He knew every hymnal.

In fact, it was the preacher of our church that was going to marry us. About two weeks before the wedding he called me and said, "Mrs. Brown, I can't do it." Somebody had threatened him and told him not to marry us.

We were later married by a man who was dressed in African apparel. He told me, "Do not look at your husband, look at me."

I said, "I'm not marrying you, I'm marrying him. I will look at whoever I want to."

I was vocal about my opinions and thoughts. I was a young spitfire at the time. I always told my husband the truth about how I felt. Those around my husband always thought I was a raspy white girl that was trying to take away their money.

My husband had money hidden all over the house, around the yard, and in the pool area.

I was locked out of the house after my husband died. After, the lawyers and the judge ordered that I was able to enter the house, I made a videotape record of everything.

With all that had gone on, with the South Carolina police, and the James Brown entourage, it didn't feel safe for me or my son. That is why I left.

In the videotape you see Mr. Bobbit's legs and Deanna Brown's hands holding a bag. I knew exactly what bag that was. It had $100,000 in it. Nobody has ever talked about that bag again. It is in the video footage, on the camera, in the court case.

They searched through the entire house for money. Later, there was almost an arrest made on Yamma Brown, but they let her go. She was sneaking around the house at night time. She was trying to dig up money.

My husband hid money everywhere because he needed to. People were stealing from him every chance they got. He was always worried about money. He used to cry in my arms and beg that God would take him. He couldn't endure the pain that so many people were stealing from him.

He would say, "I still feel like a slave. I can't live in servitude anymore." He was torn up about it.

I didn't understand this about my husband. I wondered why he didn't leave his inner circle. He could have gotten professional lawyers, professional accounting firms, and other reputable people to work for him.

He said to me, "You don't understand. You don't want to mess with this."

There is something they had over him. Later, I found out there was a blackmail issue. I think that is why he stayed with his people.

How do you blackmail James Brown, whose life is an open book? I think they knew he had done illegal things and if they turned him in to the authorities, he would have gone back to jail on a "three strikes" rule. I'm not certain. I think they were threatening him; he may have assaulted someone.

Those are my own thoughts. I don't know if that is true. I heard things discussed like that. I can't be certain. It was all very seedy. He knew it. I just get the feeling he couldn't get out.

James Brown was such a strong person. I have seen him cut people off for doing little things. I never really understood why he couldn't cut off these people who were stealing from him. There had to have been other reasons. As close as we were, there were certain things he kept private that he didn't want me to know.

My husband told me that J. Edgar Hoover opened up an investigation right after he appeared on the cover of Time magazine. Ever since then, he said that he had satellites following him. He would point to the sky and laugh about being followed. We were driving with Lady Byrd and Vicki Anderson, and he would point to the sky and say, "See up there? They (satellites) are following me. Hey Bobby – do you see that up there? They are following me!"

When he asked me about the satellites I would say to him, "It is true if you say it is true."

He challenged me, "Do you believe me?"

I responded, "I believe in you baby."

Vicki's eyes got as big as quarters. Vicki told me later, "Lord have mercy! I knew you were going to get it later when you said that!"

He was angry with me. He thought I was calling him a liar. It all seemed so unreal to me at the time. Now, I actually believe him. I absolutely do. I wished I would have believed him then, regarding all the things that were happening. It just seemed so odd to me at the time. It's not odd to me now in retrospect.

We were spied on. You could hear clicks in our bedroom. We knew we were being watched. It came out later in court that our bedroom had cameras. We didn't know about that. People were either trying to scare him into thinking he was being watched, or people were really watching. It was one or the other. I could feel it. My son could feel it. He would sometimes run out of the room because of it.

Of course, they obtained video footage of me and my husband together in our room. But they also obtained video footage of him with Gloria Daniels and Candice Hurst. I was just trying to take care of the hardest man in the world to take care of.

When the South Carolina police pulled me over, they told me they were disgusted that I had "married a nigger." I thought it was an inappropriate, racist thing to say.

They gave me a look as though I was worse than the people they were talking about because I had married "one of them."

They told me, "I would be very careful if I were you. There are a lot of places around here that people can go missing."

I challenged them on that issue.

They started to backtrack. They said, "Oh no. We are just trying to tell you that there are places out here where bad things can happen." It was all very strange that they would say such things.

When I was locked out of my house and unable to get in the home, the police would not let me in. I was holding my son's hand. They said they would not let me in without a valid marriage license. Who says those kind of things? They were told not to let me in by someone in the legal entourage. It took me six days before I could get into the house to retrieve my belongings.

Al Sharpton and the kids made it a point to leave me behind at the funeral. They left me before I could walk down 125th St. in Harlem to the Apollo Theater with my husband. When I showed up in New York they were all surprised. They didn't even know how I had made it. A friend of mine, Peter Neumann, he was a producer in New York, arranged for the flight and for guards. They tried to cut me out of the funeral procession so that it would look like I didn't want to be there.

When they came back to Augusta, they would not let me speak at the funeral. I grabbed the microphone out of Rev. Sharpton's hand and said, pointing to my husband, "That is James Brown. I am Mrs. Brown. I loved him very much."

It was something to that effect.

He grabbed the microphone away from me and said, "I was trying to be nice Tomi. No more."

I could not believe Rev. Sharpton said that to me on stage in front of so many people. We were treated horribly.

We were told not to even sit in the family section at the funeral. He asked me and my son to sit back three rows at the funeral. Mr. Bobbit was the one they had come and ask me.

He said, "Please Mrs. Brown. Please just do this." He said there were members of the entourage that would not let me sit there. They treated us horribly.

Deanna had a third or fourth funeral on her property. It was announced to me his body was going to be kept there in a crypt. She wanted to have a service that was private, away from the media, where I could be invited. It was during that service where they would be "allowed" to treat me like family. They really did me wrong, as well as their little brother. It continues to this day. I don't understand why. I was good to them.

People didn't come around my husband unless they wanted money. Al Sharpton was one of those people. They didn't want to be "right."

My husband used to say to me, "Baby they don't want to be around somebody that is going to make them 'be right."

They didn't want to address him properly; yes sir or no sir. They didn't want to speak only when spoken to. They would get their money and they would go. James Brown knew it.

Every time we were in town, without fail, he would say, "Baby, let's go for a ride." It was usually three or four times a week. We would jump in the car with a shotgun in the back seat. We would drive around and pass out $100 bills. He would pass out money to the kids. He would give out money to his old friends that he had known for decades. There was one friend who was a very poor man. He was very tall and thin. I can't remember his name but we used to drive by and give him a few hundred dollars every time we saw him.

James Brown would make the children go and get their mothers and give the money to them. He would bail people out when they were going to lose their house to foreclosure. He was always helping people. He didn't care to let everybody know what he was doing. It was private. He didn't call the press for a "photo op" so the world could see his generosity. It was his job, as the Godfather of Soul, to take care of his people. He did not want to see suffering among his people. That is how we could help them, financially.

I think giving away so much money made him feel better about himself. It relieved some of the guilt. I don't know all of the guilt that he was having for the things he had done in his life. He really was a great man. He cared so much for the little people.

He never forgot anybody's name. We would see people on the road from different countries and different cities and he would know their name. He would remember where they had spoken last. There would have been 10 or 20 years in between their last visit. He would remember everything they had talked about. He made people feel so good because he remembered them. He would recall conversations with people that never expected to be remembered. He had a great memory for people.

He was a genius with numbers. He could remember numbers, bank account numbers, phone numbers, addresses, etc. He would call all of this, "counting." He would say to me, "Baby, you have to learn how to count." It's kind of funny; my son has that very same gift. I don't know on the spectrum of genius where he exactly fell. I believe he was a savant. He could pick up any instrument and play it. He had that gift. I don't know where it comes from.

My husband would always tell me about his childhood. He told me because he wanted me to be grateful for the things that I had.

We used to take care of his mother. I used to go and brush her hair. She loved it when I would go to the nursing home with him. I would have to cuss out the nurses because they would leave her hair in ties for so long. She would have bumps on her head. She was calcium deficient and would often lie in the fetal position all cramped. Her eyes would get so big when I would come and brush her hair. She liked it when I put oils on her skin and rubbed her legs.

My husband would just laugh. He knew that his mother did not like white people. At that time in her life, she really couldn't talk. He laughed because he knew she would hate it if a white woman was rubbing her legs.

When we had our son, he was so excited to show James to his mother.

He would say to his mother, "Look mama, we got a baby together. I had a baby with a white woman, mama."

He was laughing and giggling the whole way home. He loved being able to tell her that. He knew that she was NOT going to be happy.

This story about Susie leaving James at the age of four is not true. Joe was a real bastard. She wanted out. She was ready to take the child when he pointed a gun at her and said, "You ain't taking my boy." He then started shooting at her. They would shoot at each other. James Brown would do that with one of his earlier wives as well. He was repeating the bad behaviors of his father.

They were living a life in a very different time and culture. His parents would fire off a gunshot when they were upset. They would fight and argue. They didn't have policing in the 1930s in rural South Carolina. They didn't have policing in the poor neighborhoods of Augusta in the 1940s like they do today. All of the people around James were drinking, gambling and running numbers. They all had guns and they knew how to use them. They had to engage in illegal business practices just to make money. It was just the culture and the lifestyle that people had to endure. It's very unfortunate.

Susie was a firecracker. She was tough. You had to be if you are going to be with Joe Brown.

Mr. Brown loved his daddy. That was not a joke. "Poppa Don't Take No Mess" was a song about Poppa Joe.

It had nothing to do with James Brown. It was all about his father. He was a very strict, hard-core man.

James used to get very upset with his father, however. Joe would talk so badly about white people behind their backs. Yet, when he saw a white man walking toward him down the street he would take off his hat as a sign of respect, and walk on the other side of the road. He believed that a white man would not want to have contact with a black man.

James Brown hated that. It upset him because he would be the same to a white man when he talked to his face as he would behind his back. My husband talked about that a great deal. People tell stories when they hang around each other. We are story tellers. People tend to tell the very same stories over and over again.

One of those stories he told all of the time is where Poppa Joe came from. His grandparents were slaves. He lived during Jim Crow. Black men were not equal to white men, and he felt that until the day he died. This troubled my husband. It was something that was just scarred into his memory.

I was with the band when they jumped into the pool in the Soviet republic of Georgia. My husband did whatever he wanted to do. Everybody in the band started jumping into the pool at the end of the show. It was a lot of fun. Actually, I did not jump in. Candice jumped in right after him. I was not going to jump in the pool. I had a tight dress on. I would have drowned. There is no way in that tight dress I would've been able to get out of the water. My dress was made so tight all the way down to the ankles. I would never have been able to swim. The rest of the band jumped in after him.

He did not have a fear of water like some believe. It was an amazing feat to jump into the water. He actually loved the water. But when his hair got wet it turned into "Buckwheat" - the character on The Little Rascals. That is what it was. We had a swimming pool and he loved the water. He loved to go into the ocean with friends. He didn't like what it would do to his hair. His hair always had to be pressed. Water would kink it up.

We had so much fun in Soviet Georgia. We bought so many things there. None of it arrived safely in our home back to the United States. I was very upset about it. He bought swords, gems, and other expensive things. We must've spent $100,000 while we were there. We bought so many antique pieces and they never showed up. He said to me, "Babe, those people are poor - they must have needed that money. We were never going to get that stuff."

Wow! That was not my response. In his mind, they just went to families in Georgia that need the money. What an amazing man. It was his money, it was not my money. I didn't have a right to be angry. He did and yet he wasn't. I was angry because I knew exactly where all the pieces would be placed in our home. After I overreacted, I felt ashamed of myself. Those people in Georgia were having hard-luck.

It is true. James Brown was offered millions of dollars to convert to Islam by the President Omar Bongo of Gabon. This happened several times throughout his life.

The first time it happened, all of the money was sitting there on the table. James simply walked out of the room. He said to me that he was afraid he was going to get shot, and when he walked out he wasn't sure if he was going to get out of there alive. He told them that he was not going to convert. He came into the world with his God, and hoped to leave with the very same God. This was a story that I heard him tell more than once. People on the "inside" knew the truth.

Mr. Bobbit was an advisor to the President of Gabon. The relationship with Bongo was facilitated by Bobbit. Mr. Bobbit worked with the president for many years. The president had a direct line to Mr. Brown via Mr. Bobbit.

Everybody tried to convert him. If other religions would've been able to convert him, they would've loved to have gotten their hands on James Brown.

People in the entertainment industry are always paid good money to promote a cause or a religion. Their celebrity is powerful.

When a fight is thrown, an event is fixed, or something appears to be real but is actually staged, those things are kept very quiet. It is usually between the performer and the person with the money in the room. They don't want anybody else to know what they are doing.

I was amazed at some of the things that I heard when business was conducted with my husband. I would sit quietly in the corner with my gloves off, my hat on, and dressed elegantly in blue while the men were talking business. They would talk about certain artists as though they were not even human beings; they were "disposable acts." They didn't care about the careers of these people.

James would say to me, "Sit there and be quiet. Open your eyes and your ears. Listen and learn." He was not being mean, even though what he said was stern. I learned a lot during that period of time about the business; particularly record executives.

I thought I knew a lot before I met James Brown; I didn't really know anything.

I was born in Las Vegas. I was a teenage runaway. Actually, I don't even think I made it to being a teenager. I ran away when I was nine years old. My father and my mother separated. She married a man who abused me. I used to go and knock on the door of the shelter, Child Haven, in Las Vegas. I asked them to take me in, because I did not want to sleep in my bed.

I ran away often; my mother would drag me back. I was put in foster homes, in group homes, and in all-girls Catholic homes. Any option they could think of to take care of me, they would try.

When I was 13, I told my mom that I was leaving. I ran away to Hollywood. I joined a band called "Hardly Dangerous." I told her that I was leaving to be a rock star and not to come get me. My mother was a singer in Las Vegas. She was tired of me, so she let me go. She said, "You will be dead or on the couch before you ever make it in this business." Before I knew it, I hired my mother to be my nanny and I bought her a house in South Carolina.

I was with that band for many years. We were signed by Maverick records and scheduled to perform with Madonna. The band broke up when we lost our deal with Madonna. That is when I moved to Las Vegas and started performing during the Janis Joplin Legends in Concert impersonation show.

When everything is said and done, I would like to help the girl's shelter in Las Vegas. I would like to do philanthropy work for runaway children. Without a place to run, I would not have known what to do.

Going from a runaway to being married to Mr. Brown was truly an amazing experience. I wasn't in awe of having hundreds of thousands of dollars lying around the house in cash. Mr. Brown made it so I never wanted for anything. That money wasn't mine and I didn't care because he gave me all I needed. All I had to do was ask. If he saw something wrong with me, he would get it fixed. He took very good care of me.

When I was growing up and struggling I was simply in survival mode. When I was in the band in Hollywood, we did very well. I always had a place to live. I was very lucky and had very good people around me. Many people say that I had a tough life. I don't feel like it was. I feel like I had a great time. I would not change a thing.

James Brown felt like we were destined to be together. We had similar childhoods, and we both dropped out of school when we were very young. I believe I may have unknowingly drawn him to me – the law of attraction.

Before I met James Brown, I was in Las Vegas. I was training my voice for the Janis Joplin audition. I was listening to James Brown and Janis Joplin records. They have similar voices. My best friend asked me who I was listening to. I told her I was listening to James Brown. I brought the CD to her; she thought I was listening to a girl. I showed her the cover and she said, "God. He is the ugliest black man I have ever seen in my life."

I told her not to say that. I told her he was absolutely beautiful; this was James Brown, The Godfather of Soul.

She asked me if I would ever marry him.

I said that I would absolutely marry him and "have his baby!"

One year later it all started to happen. That is a true story. I prayed for him to come to me. Maybe the good Lord knew James Brown needed somebody – and I needed somebody. I think I just opened the door in a way that I don't fully understand.

James Brown was able to stop the rain. We would be in the middle of a downpour. We would need to hit the stage in minutes. He would say to me, "Don't worry, the sun is going to come out." Naturally, the sun would come out.

Anybody that really knew James Brown will tell you he had some kind of special psychic ability. He could tell things and he could see things. He would make those things happen. He was blessed in that specific way, although I don't really know what it was.

I understood from the very beginning that James Brown was a man of destiny. I understood he was placed on this earth to change the world. I knew of his greatness. That is why I was not troubled by his demons. All of the other things in his life were insignificant compared to the good he had done. He needed to take care of himself (sexually) in such a way as to continue with the strength needed to complete his work. Who was I to call that into question? Let the man have a little joy if that is where he finds it.

I never once considered James Brown to be an adulterer. He was a good man to me. He never made me feel like there was any other woman in our relationship unless he wanted to make me jealous. Sometimes he wanted me to show him more affection. I don't think he was an adulterer in the sense that people should be condemning him. It was more complicated than that. You had to have a sense of maturity about who he was.

I did not get to perform with the band when James Brown sang with Pavarotti. I was pregnant during that time; I was behind the scenes. It was an incredible experience. Every time we would go to Monte Carlo, in the South of France, it was always so beautiful. The people there love him so much. Singing with Pavarotti was beautiful, it was magical.

My husband could work, sing with, and perform brilliantly with so many people; he was simply amazing. He had such broad talent. He was such a great entertainer. James Brown was every bit the vocalist that Pavarotti was. He would walk around the house and sing opera just like Pavarotti. He could actually sing like that. He could do whatever he wanted with his voice.

He was an amazing singer and an amazing writer. We would work together at the studio when we returned from performing on the road. The studio was available to use at our disposal.

I have many recordings that nobody has ever heard. I have many songs where we were just putting the beat down and "barking" lyrics. We wrote a song called, "Killing is Out, School Is In" that we took all the way to President Bush. It was just something he had an idea for one day. "Killing is out. School is in. I don't think you heard me brother, say it again…try romance, turn that cap around and take that gun out of your pants." We sang that song with Bobby Byrd. The song was talking about all of these children taking guns to school. He would come up with those lyrics in one second. He was amazing like that.

I was in the car with him when he would talk to young kids on the wrong side of the tracks. Their pants were hanging below their butts and their ball caps were facing backwards. He said, "Whatever direction your hat is facing, that is where you are going in life. If you want to go backwards or forwards that is where you are headed. Pull your pants up where your grades ought to be. Put your cap and your life facing forward."

The day we got married he looked at my eyes and said, "I never realized how beautiful you were to me until this very moment." It took my breath away, it melted my heart. James Brown was not a man who would often say tender things. That was a very tender moment for me because he was such a guarded person. He protected his emotions. He said that in front of everyone who attended the wedding in our home.

James Brown would play people against each other. For example (completely hypothetical), he might say to me: "Tomi, I can't trust that Buddy Dallas. I think he's stealing from me."

And then he would approach Buddy and say, "Mr. Dallas, Tomi Rae is just trouble. I think she is stealing from me."

He would do that all of the time. He would do it just for fun. He would pit people against each other. He would do it with the band. He used to call it a very specific name: "Sabotage." Everybody in the band knew exactly what it was. Ask the band if they knew about Sabotage. James Brown was usually behind the problem. He was just a little troublemaker.

He was the master of his own world. He would move the people in his life, the pieces in his life, just like a master playing on a chessboard. He loved to move pieces around. I used to sit back and watch what he would do, and just laugh and pray that I was not going to be the next victim. I was the victim many times. I can laugh about it now; not so much then.

That is also how he got information. He would make people feel like they were with him; not the other person. He used to find out a lot of information by being nice to people.

James Brown said his son Teddy was definitely murdered for being with white women in a car while on a trip to Toronto. There was evidence showing the black men in the car were attacked and the white women were left alone. When you looked at the accident, the dead bodies were the evidence. The white women were not touched, or something to that effect. He told me that somebody had come and bashed the black men's heads in after the fact. That is what he believed. It tore him apart. He loved Teddy.

When we went and had the sonogram done, he thought we were going to have a girl. He wanted to have a boy like Teddy. He didn't care what I was going to name her if it was a girl. When he found out it was a boy he did that thing where you jump up in the air and click your heels together.

He said, "We got a boy. We made a boy. We're going to have a boy! If you are going to have a girl, it's the woman's job to name the child. If you're going to have a boy, it's the man's job to name the child. We are going to have a boy and it will be my job to name the child."

From that moment on, I didn't have anything to say about the name of my child; he would be named James Joseph Brown II.

"Baby, those are big shoes to fill. I don't think we should call him James Brown. It will be rough for this kid." He said to me, "Baby, you don't know what I know. This boy is going to do more than I ever did. He will have my name and he will be half white. This kid can be the President of the United States." All right. That was it. James Brown II he is.

He doted on that child. He loved him. I believe that his spirit is around him today. I can feel him close by. Young James can feel him as well. I believe he is stuck to my son's side.

When I feel his presence near me, I talk to him out loud. I ask him to forgive me. I have so much guilt for not being with him the last month of his life. Sometimes I wish he would hold me. Sometimes I'm mad at him. I get angry because of all we had to go through regarding his will. The hardest times I have had in my life was after he passed away. I have struggled. I have raised my son on my own. I have never had another job other than as a performer. Because I have been so publicly humiliated, it has been hard for me to even get a job. Sometimes I get mad at James Brown, because I can't take care of his child.

Mr. Bobbit's told me, and he has told others by way of affidavit, that James Brown's last words out of his mouth were, "Mr. Bobbit, take care of my wife and little man."

During one of the funerals, Charles Bobbit was finishing his remarks. I had just walked into the room. Some of the girls got up and stomped out. Bobbit looked at me and said to all that were there, "I'm sorry, but I have to say this right now. I promised my brother James that whenever I saw her, I would acknowledge his wife as Mrs. Brown and his son as James Brown II." He said that in front of everybody.

You could feel and hear the scoffing in the room. People were saying and thinking, "What is she doing here?"

Mr. Bobbit made me feel a lot better when he told me that those were James' last words. Mr. Bobbit has done his very best to take care of us. He has sent money when he can afford to do so. He has called me to see how we are doing. Mr. Bobbit has definitely tried to extend a helping hand.

Vicki Anderson has told me that James Brown was in the car with her, her husband Bobby Byrd, and Charles Bobbit when he said, "I want 17.5% of all of my residual income to go to Tomi Rae." We had documents to prove that. Unfortunately, when they went into my house, we had a wall safe behind a picture. I wouldn't have noticed it, but the picture changed.

When I went into the room I asked, "Why is that picture different?"

The safe was missing. The walls were boarded up like the rest of the wood behind the picture. The safe had been there for many years. It had all of the wills, house deeds, and other important documents. It came out in court that there were other wills. Nobody knew where they were. That is because they were in the stolen safe. They took it from the house when they locked me out for those six days.

The lawyers and the kids went all through the house. They took whatever they wanted. It was ransacked by the time I was able to enter six days later. I went through the house with a video camera and recorded everything. We had a big safe in the house. Somebody had taken a sledgehammer and tried to break in. Someone had tried to drill through the safe and they couldn't get it open. The safe contained all of my jewelry and his as well.

Today, my son and I are struggling. We sleep on couches that belong to friends. I have been wiped out of money. People talk about loving him, but they knew he would not approve of this treatment of either me or my son. They had Mr. Brown's legs cut open and the bone taken out just to test this little boy. I said to that person:

"Do you mean to tell me that you are going to cut out the Godfather's legs, just so you could test his DNA? You know he loves this little boy. You know he loves his son."

I held James Brown's hand when they cut open his legs with the bone-saw. They needed to extract bone marrow, because he was embalmed so quickly after death.

They didn't want me to order an autopsy. In fact, Yamma Brown signed the death certificate and had Adrienne as the widow. I had to get a court order to have the death certificate changed. I am now listed as the widow. She had to do all of that to have him embalmed so quickly.

Deanna Brown was angry with me.

She said, "I know what you are doing because it took me two hours to clean up the room with all the stuff (drugs) on the floor."

I responded, "Really? How long did it take you to dirty up mine?"

She just looked at me and walked away. I don't know exactly what was in the room. I know it was a mess – I have been told my husband was doing drugs. Along with the mess, they took money, jewelry, clothing, awards, pictures, and a lot of memorable things.

This was cruel. I did not understand how they could have the right to limit my access to the home where I had lived for years. They attended our wedding ceremony in the home. I was not some in and out woman that he kept.

Throughout our entire marriage, and for decades previous, the children were not allowed access to the home. They were not allowed near the kitchen, bedroom - nothing. Rarely, were they allowed passed the foyer. The children and the trustees did not even let me retrieve my personal things. Rather, they sent my belongings in crates. What they don't understand – or maybe they do – it was James that wanted it that way. He had limited the children's access to him, to his home, and to his money – not me.

It was the women that made it most difficult for me, particularly the women in the band. I know some of the white men could not believe that I was there for any other reason but to take James Brown's money. I know that. That is simply not why I was there. I just loved the man. I thought I could help him be on earth a little bit longer.

***

The other side of the story is told by those of James Brown's inner circle.

Rita Udom

Mr. Brown was like family to me. He would come into my home and help himself to whatever was in the refrigerator. He would lie down in my daughter's bedroom before flying out for a show. I would always tell him not to mess with drugs. I knew that a lot of people who came around him were giving him drugs. I knew that Tomi Rae was his primary source of drugs.

Tomi Rae did not really care for him. It was unfortunate that she ever came into his life. When he really needed her, she was never there. There were times when I asked him to call his wife. She was never around.

I believe I met her for the first time in Reno Nevada. She was playing roulette. The next time I saw her I asked, "Who is SHE?" Mr. Brown told me that she had given him a demo CD. She was flirting with him. She had tattoos on her body. She looked cheap. She was not polished. I asked all of Mr. Brown's entourage, "What is she hanging around here for?" I was protective of him. I didn't want him around drugs. I didn't want him around crazy women.

I took care of all of his medical issues. His girls could not have any venereal diseases or issues associated with drugs. I told him he could not have any contact with drugs. That is why I am so opposed to Tomi Rae. The last year of his life she left him and took all of his money. He had a habit of going to the bank and withdrawing $100,000. Sometimes he would withdraw $300,000. He would call me and tell me that the money was missing. He didn't know if it had been taken. She was taking a lot of his money.

He brought Tomi Rae's baby to me twice. He wanted me to do a DNA analysis. The last time he came, I did not have the correct kit. I regret not having that DNA kit close at hand.

I asked him, "Where is Tomi Rae?"

He said, "She is doing her nails." I have never heard of a lady do her nails so often. I think she was out doing drugs.

One time, he said he was going to put me in his will. I told him not to do that. I knew it was going to be a mess. Nobody that he intended to receive money has benefited from the will. Please tell me, who sets up a legal will, where the actions are not carried out? He wanted to make sure that Tomi Rae had no part in his will. She was a gold-digger. I reminded him how I felt about her when they met. She needs to be forced to have a DNA test on that child.

Mr. Brown came to my house and asked me to listen to her CD. He said she sounded like Janis Joplin.

I told him, "This CD does not sound anything like Janis Joplin. She is just a gold-digger. She needs to go to rehab."

He said to me, "Oh give her a chance, give her a chance."

She knew how to control him with drugs. She was a major drug whore. That was the only way to get money out of James Brown.

One day, Tomi Rae told me that the South Carolina police stopper her. She asked them why they were giving her a ticket. She thought she might have been speeding.

They said, "Oh we're not giving you a ticket. We want to know why you're married to that monkey."

They told her, "We are going to kill that monkey you are married to!"

I asked her if she told Mr. Brown what she was telling me. She said, "No." I told her that she knew they were going to try to kill Mr. Brown. Why didn't she share that with him? That is the kind of person she is. I knew that the South Carolina police wanted to kill him.

***

Buddy Dallas

There is also the issue of his would-be wife. She is no more his wife than any strange woman off the street. Tomi Rae Hynie was married to a man from Pakistan. Mr. Brown was so hurt and embarrassed by this. Mr. Brown was "old school."

Mr. Brown loved women. He would, however, respect your wife. He would respect you as her husband. He would never, never consider making an advance on your wife. If he found that a woman was married that was making a

112

move toward him, he would say to her, "Ma'am, you need to go home to your husband."

David Cannon

He would call my wife and talk to her about Adrienne. In my opinion, if the Devil ever walked on this earth, it was in the form of that woman. That was her. Then, with his last woman, his so-called wife, Tomi Rae, he would call my wife and asked her to take Tomi Rae out shopping. He wanted her to go buy things. He wanted Tomi Rae to be around my wife more so she could learn to act like a lady. That was the kind of relationship my wife and I had with the man.

Mr. Brown had a couple of three problems. The first was radio stations. The second was cars, and the third problem he had, was young white women. Before he supposedly married Tomi Rae, we were at the radio station from 3:30 PM to 6 PM. I was trying to get him not to marry Tomi Rae. He wanted to marry her because it would look good.

I said to him, "Mr. Brown, if you want a young white woman on your arm, I will buy you one. If that's what you want." I told him not to marry her.

Of course, she was married to somebody else when she married him. The marriage was ultimately dissolved.

Final thoughts

Tomi Rae said she never saw my father beat a woman. I hope for her sake that is true. It does not appear to be the case.

2003 was a difficult year for the couple. 2004 started off worse.

In June of 2003, someone from my father's office placed a beautiful family picture of my father standing next to a much taller Goofy. Tomi Rae was dressed beautifully on his left, James Brown II was standing in front, his attention clearly directed somewhere else. Cinderella's Castle was in the background – an odd irony if you think about Tomi Rae.

The picture was sent to Variety Magazine with these words. "Due to Mr. James Brown and Mrs. Tomi Rae Brown's heavy demanding tour schedule, they have decided to go their separate ways. "We both love each other, but it has become difficult to function together.....

Mr. & Mrs. James Brown."

They remained together after the publication, and performed jointly on a regular basis. Who was responsible for this announcement? The reference to Tomi Rae as Mrs. Brown is interesting. Tomi Rae had informed my father earlier that year that she had been fraudulently married to another man. That marriage was annulled.

In 2004, my father pleaded "no contest" to a domestic violence charge. He was not required to serve any additional jail time. The original police report disclosed that Tomi Rae suffered "scratches and bruises to her right arm and hip." The infamous mug-shot was paraded nationally and internationally, mocking my father's hair, beard, and clothing.

Of course, there was more to the story.

Power had been lost throughout the entire region for three days. An ice-storm had hit Augusta. My father's home did not have power. He and Tomi Rae were going stir crazy. On the third day they started to fight. Brown chased Tomi Rae inside the house – and threw an iron chair at her. The police report said she had scratches on her hip and arm. Others who saw her wounds disagree.

What is clear is Tomi had been abused as a young girl. That fact is well known. The fight triggered an emotional response that restored her childhood memories and mental anguish. Her self-defense mechanism was to call 911.

She hung up the phone immediately but the connection to dispatch had been made. My father was arrested and released the next morning. She was taken away in an ambulance and quickly released from the hospital. Interestingly, they both seemed to regret the incident.

My father was encouraged to completely separate from Tomi and get a DNA test on the child to prove a lack of paternity. He refused. He said that he was not going to

115

harm either one. He knew that they would sort the mess out after his death.

The case was settled for a simple fine. Given my father's lengthy history of drug and spouse abuse, jail time would be certain. However, the court was made aware of the facts and lack of physical harm. Brown had exceptional lawyers but really did not need them. Tomi Rae was not interested in pushing the prosecution for obvious reasons.

Charles Bobbit provided a quote from my father to GQ magazine that frames the rocky relationship quite differently:

"I am going to marry her again. She is my wife. I love her. I ain't going to punish her no more."

Bobbit has also said on many occasions that the dying words of James Brown were, "I want you to look after my wife…and little man."

I am not aware that Mr. Bobbit has retracted those words.

I had a very different experience with my father regarding Tomi Rae.

One morning we were taking my father to the dentist in Atlanta. David Washington and I were driving his Mercedes with a large mobile phone attached to the center console. That morning, my father had locked Tomi Rae out of the house and put her clothes in the front yard. He called Buddy Dallas on the phone to inform him that he wanted her out of the house. They discussed other legal matters

116

that I didn't fully understand. Tomi Rae called the car phone. My father answered and put the call on speaker by accident. We did our very best to look straight forward pretending that we could not hear a single screaming word. My father was giving her the business, and then Tomi Rae screamed, "You black mother fucker!" That ended that call.

Picture this – my father was not going to let his wife talk to him like that. It would have been a sign of male weakness had he not responded. He had "his boys" in the car with him. I was trying not to laugh hysterically. My stomach started to hurt as well as my lips and teeth as I was clinching them so tight. I could not let my father see my laugh; he would have whipped my ass and I was a grown man! My father got that dark look in his eyes. He turned around to David, who didn't dare make eye contact.

He dialed Tomi Rae's number and said, "I know what your problem is…you need your Dildo!" He quickly hung-up the phone.

I had to stop at a gas station to run away from my father as quickly as I could. I don't remember laughing that hard in my entire life.

Nice comeback dad.

Stallions & Thoroughbreds

Brown used to call his women, 'stallions!' or thoroughbreds. Stallions had small ankles and thoroughbreds had thick ankles. "Look at all the horses - let's go for a ride." I heard him say that more than once. I didn't have the heart to tell him a stallion was a male horse. He liked the sound of the word "staaaaallions" as it came from his raspy throat. I never had the heart to try to correct the man.

***

My father loved sex and he loved women. I am certain he knew very little about either. He had a huge…sense of humor when it came to sex.

My father would say, "I did a nickel last night." That means he had five orgasms. It did not mean he had five women. It would just make me laugh. I don't know if I ever took him seriously. He would never say, "I did a trey or a triple." It was always, I mean always, "a nickel." He was just talking junk.

There are only two people that know this: My father was afraid of the dark. He was frightened to be by himself. He was always left in the dark as a little child. Pop would leave him alone. Something terrible happened to my father as a young boy. I wish I knew the details. All I know is he was afraid. It all started with Barnwell.

118

He had to have a woman next to him every night. While minds may wander about his sexual exploits, please understand that my father wanted - no, needed - a warm body next to him, as much as he wanted another sexual conquest. A warm body brought him continued comfort. Sex provided extreme ecstasy. He wanted and needed both.

His bedroom might as well have had a revolving door. In AND out. When he was done, you were done. His "stallions" would return to a separate bedroom if they were staying in his home. While on the road, his "traveling" companions would always have their own room. The Godfather needed to have options and he needed to maintain control. He also needed to get things done during the night - that was when he was most productive. He was on fire. His clock always seemed backwards to me.

Brown insisted - I mean insisted - that a woman on his arm must always look the part while in public. Rather than viewed as a sexual commodity for consumption, she was an investment in future record sales. There were times when my father would spend tens of thousands of dollars on a woman, just to get the right look. Dad was certain that a young beautiful woman would enhance his public image. Extravagance, opulence, superficial beauty - it all sells. Younger audiences were dropping dollars for James Brown, and in part, it was because they perceived he had mastered the art of sexual conquest. That wasn't what was really happening. The woman on his arm was about ROI - return on investment! It was about cash.

As for me, my father wasn't around very often. Bea Ford, my mother, was. Even though I lived near my father for three years in Augusta, my sense of a proper relationship with a woman came from my mother. James Brown did not have that blessing. If you have a good relationship with your mother, you will know how to be a good family man. He didn't have that. I don't excuse his behavior - but I do understand it.

I will never forget the advice my father gave me about women. We were on the road. I was young. He told me right to my face, "If you have a girl, you need to go and get your own room." He said it in the presence of Danny Ray and Uncle Henry Stallings.

When we finished a show in San Francisco, Uncle Stallings went down to the front desk to get the hotel bill. We were on the plane together and my father became very stern. James Brown held the bill up to my face and with a harsh tone said, "What's this?"

We were staying at the Sheraton. He knew everything when it came to money. He knew all of the figures in his head. He was asking me why I wanted to get my own hotel room.

Uncle Stallings told my dad, "Daryl had to go get his own room. He had a guest."

First of all, you know my dad couldn't say NOTHING! He started to say something. My Uncle Henry stood up for me.

He said, "James, that's what you told him to do."

My father turned around and said to me, "Son, you know what your problem is? You like too many women."

That was coming from him! What saved me is that he told me to get a room when all of the men were together. That happened 40 years ago and I remember it as though it were yesterday.

I once had a woman contact me on Myspace. She said she was my sister. She said she didn't want anything. Her mother was white. If you look at this girl, although she had glasses, she looked exactly like me. All she wanted to do was say hello. My mother saw the same picture and asked me if I called my sister back. She thought it was my sister that I had known for years. It wasn't. It was this other girl. Things like that happen when you deal with James Brown.

You need to understand - James Brown was a player! He may have had a wife, but he also had his girls. You could take one woman to the airport, to drop her off, and pick up another arriving on a different flight. You can take a woman down the escalator and a woman was coming up to go straight into his room. He did not like to be by himself.

"Papa's got a brand-new bag". You knew what he was trying to say when you heard the song. I don't need to tell you. If I tell you, you weren't listening to the song.

"Come here sister. Papa's in the swing." "Body Heat" was another song. It was all about him being alone. He needed to have a body lying next to him. That's how it was. "So take a look at those cakes" is a line in one of his songs. He loved big butts! "Cakes" were big butts. Take notice - he never used profanity in his songs. His songs were left up to interpretation by design.

James Brown was the type of guy who loved women for one thing, but hated them for another. The relationship was always on his terms. He used them for companionship. I knew that when he was with certain women, women that I knew, it was going to be a good day. If they were around for a week, it was going to be a good week. He was just that way. These special women were not there just for sex. They were there for a lot of reasons. He was never by himself.

Ms. Daniels and Ms. Johnson were two women he really cared about. They were kept women. He did all he could to take care of them financially. Gloria was beautiful, but ghetto. She had a terrible mouth and a terrible mind. Ms. Johnson took very good care of him - she really loved him. Unfortunately, she did not fit the public image he needed. She was a simple woman.

My dad was not into kinky sex. He didn't know very much about sex. He came to me one time and said, "Man! They got this TV channel called The Playboy Channel." He said, "Son, women don't need us anymore. They have got this thing called a dildo." It made me laugh. He was just learning about sex for the first time - as an old man!

I was now becoming uncomfortable because I knew at any moment I was going to start laughing hysterically at Mr. Sex Machine.

Mr. (I did me a nickel last night) Dynamite said, "What about the 69 thing?"

I told him that was great.

He said to me, "No! I do 68."

But he was James Brown. He was old school. He was always on top - missionary style. That's all he knew; it was hilarious!

For years I thought he was a raging bull. That is what he told everyone. During his infamous interview with Sonya on CNN he proclaimed, "I'm single and I want to mingle. I look good, I smell good, I feel good, and I make love good!" Of course he was high. Sonya quickly changed the subject to the religious magazine he was publishing out of Augusta, Georgia. "The Second Coming," he said. He didn't miss a beat.

I remember a time when he was performing in California and told the entire crowd he had "Bull testicles." He must've been high. They called me at 12:30 AM East

Coast time. He was on the West Coast. I told them how to get him calmed down. I wasn't going to come out to California and babysit the man.

I thought he was the Godfather of Soul and the Godfather of Sex. Not so. James Brown did not know what the Playboy Channel was. He just found it surfing with the remote one day. I told him there were many adult stations. He had no idea. It was funny to me. The way he acted - I thought to myself he was great in bed. I thought he knew everything. He didn't know nothing! Women wanted to be with him and they threw themselves at him. He never had to earn it. He never had to do nothing that brought them pleasure - it was all for him.

He really liked women with big butts. "Look at those cakes!" We all knew what that meant. He loved his women thick. He loved the look of Jennifer Lopez, J-LO. He liked full figured singers. He had his eye on a particular singer that was a full-figured woman but would not discuss it further. He respected her and she later married.

William Murrell was a good friend and trusted employee for my father. It was his job to pick up the girls wherever they were and bring them to my father. They came from all over the world and had different ethnic backgrounds. He liked white girls, black girls, Asian, European, it really didn't matter. He didn't see in color - he saw in sex. Often they were much younger, but he had his stable of horses that had been around for years.

Many of his women loved the time, attention, and money he spent on them. Unfortunately, they did not know when their time was up. Some of them thought they could move into the home. The fact is, they needed simply to move along. Dad was good about arranging for William to take them home or to the airport – but some thought sex meant love. That was not what it was about for my father.

***

William Murrell

Brown is like that. He stays away from his kids. "It's a man's world, not a kid's world." In his house, in Brown's bedroom, nobody stays there all night. In his house you have your own room that you would spend the night in. Once you finish taking care of business in his room, you would go back to your room. You don't stay in his room all night.

If he was going to make love to you, you make love in his room, and then you go back to your room. Seriously. That is the way he did it. I have driven all of these girls to the airport. He had two girls at the house at the very same time. They stayed in their own little room. They stayed in their space. When they leave, that's it. Over.
I took this one girl to the airport. She was the prettiest girl. Oh man, she was beautiful. I wanted her for myself! He gave her $5000 just to spend the night with him. She didn't stay in his room all night. She did stay at the house all

night. He was a man! I don't think he ever slept. He was 24/7.

The girls would get back in the car and they would fall asleep on the way to the airport. I'm serious. I would ask them, "What's wrong?"

They said, "I didn't sleep at all last night." This man would keep them up all night long.

I took the girls to the house and back to the airport. One would be leaving town and the other would be coming in – all at the very same time! The women would pass each other in the airport and they wouldn't even know otherwise. All the girls were different. He had some pretty girls too.

I fell in love with one of the girls. She was from Atlanta. I wish I could see her again. She was a young beautiful girl. She had a Coca-Cola body. What made it so nice about her, is that she had her own money. This girl drove a Jaguar. She stayed in a real nice house in Alpharetta Georgia. You have to have money to stay in Alpharetta Georgia - all of the entertainer's stay in the same neighborhood in Georgia.

This girl had a big, four-bedroom house. It was like a mansion. She was very intelligent. She was single with no kids. She smelled sweet - just like a fruitcake. Mr. Brown would call me when she was finished and he would say, "Come pick her up, I'm finished with her." I would pick her up and come take her home. Remember, I was on call 24/7.

I would get calls at 3AM or 4AM: "Mr. Murrell, I need you right away."

I'm not telling you what I've heard; I'm telling you what I've done. I was there. That happened a lot. Particularly when he had been on tour and he would come home and wanted to spend some quality time with the ladies.

He would say to me, "Mr. Murrell, a man is not supposed to be alone. He is always supposed to have a woman." This is an agreement that you have to have with your wife. It was just something you had to have. His wives understood it. He would have his wife and a girl in the house at the same time.

When you were in his house you would do business in his bedroom and then you would go out when you are done. He had a big TV in the ceiling of his room. He had a huge TV in the ceiling of the roof and one on the wall.

He was the Godfather. One-of-a-kind. What he says goes. And the girls listen to them. He would say to me, "Mr. Murrell, the girls got on their knees and crawled to me last night."

I said, "What!"

He said, yes sir, she was on her knees as she crawled all up to me."

***

Dr. Rita Udom - **Personal physician and long-time friend**

Mr. Brown would always send his girlfriends to me to have them checked out medically. Many of them, I would send back to the airport after examining them. They had drugs in their system or they had other medical issues that would not be good for his health. He trusted me to check them out. I would call him and tell him that I already sent a girl back to the airport.

When James Brown came out of prison, I went to Japan to first do a show. None of the doctors in this area would see him because of the public perception regarding James Brown. I knew what was going on. I took care of all of his medical issues. His girls could not have any venereal diseases or issues associated with drugs. I told him he could not have any contact with drugs. That is why I am so opposed to Tomi Rae.

Candice Hurst

Tomi Rae had a relationship with James Brown the very same way all of the other wives did. That was unfortunate. I did not.

James Brown considered Tomi Rae his wife; his legal wife. He gave her hell. Honestly, people say she was the one who lasted the longest. I think I lasted longer. At the end of his life she was gone so much. Mr. Brown really needed a companion. He absolutely considered her his wife. Unfortunately, he treated her like one of his wives. It was not the best.

The relationship between the two of us evolved. In addition to being my boss, we became friends and the last three years we were intimate. It wasn't my "job" to be with Mr. Brown when Tomi Rae was gone. It was not a job. It was not her decision. She did not know about our relationship until the very last year of Mr. Brown's life. I was the one that told her. The first two years I did not share that detail with her. My relationship with Mr. Brown had nothing to do with Tomi Rae.

Naturally, there were many women from his past. Unlike others, I did his hair. I did his makeup. I woke him up in the morning and I put him into bed at night, even if Tomi Rae was there. Please understand, yes we were close, but he was my friend more than anything. Yes, there were other women in James Brown's life and Tomi Rae knew that. I would always let James Brown be James Brown.

James Brown and I had a blast together. We had so much fun. I was his upper. God, music, and Mr. Brown saved my life.

Just like the band, James Brown had to have two of everything.

***

Buddy Dallas

Mr. Brown loved women. He would, however, respect your wife. He would respect you as her husband. He would never consider making an advance on your wife. If he found that a woman was married and was making a move toward him he would say to her, "Ma'am, you need to go home to your husband." He respected the marriage relationship. I always appreciated that he felt this way about married women. Now, if the woman wasn't married, that was a whole different ballgame.

Mr. Brown was not going to spend the night alone. He was never, I mean never, going to spend the night alone. There was a particular, attractive lady from Israel. He would send the Concorde jet for her. He would bring her over for a weekend, and then send her back to Israel. I have seen Mr. Brown send a woman out the back door when another was arriving at the front door. He had an insatiable appetite for women. Women had in insatiable appetite for James Brown. They pursued him.

Mr. Brown was a born leader. I asked him once to tell me about "Sex Machine." I asked him what had prompted that song. He said, "I was just trying to get people to get up and dance like a sex machine. That was my only intention. I simply wanted to get people to get up and dance."

***

David Cannon

Women around James Brown would talk to my wife. We traveled together quite often. They would hear terrible things about Mr. Brown's wife Adrienne.

They would then ask my wife, "What kind of man is James Brown?"

She would say, "He is probably the most gentle man I have ever seen. I have never seen him act toward me or anybody else in a lack of a gentlemanly way. He is a gracious person."

He liked young white women. We were in Los Angeles and we saw a young 18 or 19 year-old woman at the place we were having lunch. She had the chance to meet him at the show the night before. We were sitting around the table and I did not know who she was. She introduced herself to me. Al Sharpton was on the other side with Mr. James Brown. I saw Mr. Brown elbow Mr. Sharpton and then point to the young woman.

He said to me, "Mr. Cannon, this is my new wife. I met her last night."

I just sat there with my mouth open. My wife was sitting next to me and she didn't know what to say. Neither of us could say a word. He waited for about two or three minutes and he started laughing.

He said, "I knew you wouldn't like that."

You need to understand that women were all part of Mr. Brown's game plan. As old as he was, if he had a beautiful younger woman on his arm, he knew people would buy his music. People don't buy old man's music. In a sense, the women were investments.

***

Relationships were not always clean and simple with my father. Decisions he made regarding his marriage made life complex. Hollie Farris captured the volatility of these relationships without knowing the details of what was going on at home. This story comes from an earlier wife - but it was typical of all of his married relationships. Hollie remembers,

"I will never forget the first show I ever did with him. It was in Mexico City, Mexico. He was wearing a white jumpsuit. He did a couple of knee drops and I looked over and all I could see were bloodstains on his knees. Blood was soaking through his pants! I thought to myself, 'Man - oh man - this guy is something! He makes his knees bleed every show!' As it turned out, he had just been in a fight with his wife a few days before. He reached in the car window and grabbed her by the hair as she was driving away. She rolled up the electric window on his arm and dragged him down the driveway. His legs were dangling on the road.

That was my very first gig with James Brown. I had no idea what I was in for. I don't think that story has ever been told."

Section II
The Music, Inside and Out

On January 1, 1969, James Brown made a memorable, if not historic, appearance on the Mike Douglas Show. Brown was nothing short of masterful. Douglas concluded the day almost reverently,

"Some talk to blacks. Some talk to whites."

Brown interrupted as if he had written the script,

"I talk to people."

The music of James Brown transcends race, creed, color, genre and time. He often said his music was "20 years ahead of its time." His music is timeless. His life, a gift to the world. My father said, "Of all the music in the world today, 80% is influenced by James Brown."

Stevie Wonder believed the number was too small.

A British Journalist in 1987 asked,

"Was it always your ambition to be a singer?"

He cocked his head and looked her right in the eyes, "My ambition was to eat! We were very hungry. We were very poor people. Singing and music was the way I was able to earn a living."

Brown continued, "We were living in a home with 19 people and the rent was only $5 a month. The adults could not get it. I went and danced for the soldiers and made $12 – they had the rent for two months. That is what music meant for me. I was able to go and make a decent life for myself. God gave me the talent and the vision to make me independent in my music."

Naturally, he had been telling this story for years.

Soul, Funk, R&B…Brown defined and continually refined them all. His music is rhythmically brilliant - as though it penetrated past the cellular level and transformed human DNA.

He said, "Soul is something that is spiritual. You don't know what you are going to get into. Soul just happens. Soul is a feeling. Soul is life. Soul is everyday movement – it is what we feel…God has all control of movement and what we do on stage."

Previously, most music had been written on the upbeat: on the 2 and 4. Brown changed all of that. It was now on the down beat: "On the One" and three. To not be moved by James Brown means you can't be moved.

Sidney Miller was correct:

"Just remember one thing. James Brown's band has always been known as the cleanest non-drug band in the world. Before his band could go on stage, James Brown had an inspection. Everybody would line up. They were not allowed to smoke a goddamn cigarette. They were not allowed to drink anything before they went on stage. He smelled their breath. He made sure their shirt was clean and starched and their shoes were shined. All of these things were a part of the rules of playing with James Brown."

The band was made out of unbelievably talented people. Bootsy Collins may be the finest bass player of all time. Mousey, Spike, Hollie, Leroy, Keith, and Fred; all of them were spectacular.

My father was hard on the band – but he loved them. If the band hadn't performed for a few weeks he would bring them to Augusta for rehearsal. Nobody in the band needed to rehearse with James Brown. They knew his music perfectly - but they did need to put food on the table and pay the mortgage. Brown wanted to take care of them, but he also wanted them to earn their keep.

The following reflections are provided by several members of the band. Two memorable events are highlighted: a performance in Georgia (the former Soviet satellite) and the epic performance of Man's, Man's, Man's, world with Pavarotti.

***

Hollie Farris

I was performing with a show band from Nashville, at a hotel in Atlanta, where James used to stay when he was in town. Our band was playing in the lounge when James Brown came in and heard us. He liked what he heard, and after a brief conversation, hired me on the spot. Later on, he hired two other players from that same band, on my recommendation of course. It was a case of being in the right place at the right time.

I stayed with Mr. Brown for eight years and then I quit after a series of bad experiences. I returned to the band after he left prison and then stayed with him another 16 years, for a total of 24 years.

The fines were legendary. By legendary, I mean they occurred primarily in the 1960s. I joined the band around 1975. By this time, he was not fining the band nearly as often. However, every now and then, if you really screwed up, he would start flashing his hand with his fingers extended toward you. It was five dollars, then five more. If you weren't watching him, the dollars would quickly add up and he would fine you for 10 minutes straight. You had to stay on your toes. You absolutely had to watch him at all times. You never knew what he was going to do or when he was going to do it.

Mr. Brown was a taskmaster when it came to rehearsing. One would expect his songs to be just like the records, but that was not always the case. He would change the songs. He would try new things out. He was throwing chasers and riffs and would incorporate other things that were not on the record. He was always trying different things.

Because of this complexity, his band became indispensable. You could not try that with a studio band. You could not try that with new players. They had to be familiar with each other, completely familiar. He trained his band to do just that. You didn't always know what was coming. You needed to feel it; you had to have a sense of what was coming. You had to anticipate what might happen and then catch it when he delivered. It was training like no other band I had been in before. You had to be on top of your game at all times. You could not slack off for a minute.

This seamless relationship made for a tight show. It taught us discipline. Many bands just get up there and are sloppy. They don't invest all of themselves. Not the band that performed with Mr. Brown. That would never have been acceptable. It was "all" or "none." He could pick up on that. He heard it. He knew if you were not giving your very best. If you were not willing to play your best, you had to go find a new job.

For Mr. Brown, the band was central to his success. Everything we did was a show. The band was integral - from our music to our wardrobe. It was not possible to expend that amount of energy for two hours straight. He needed to rely on us to catch his breath and recover. He couldn't dance for two straight hours every show. It was not possible to perform at the level James Brown wanted to perform, without taking a quick rest. Have you seen his dancing, his energy? It was legendary.
In some sense, the performance was a circus. He had singers, dancers, and the band. It really was a three-ring circus. You never knew what you were going to get. Every show was different. Mr. Brown might call on a different

soloist to perform. He even had a magician at one time. Nobody ever got the same show twice.

The show really was spontaneous. He felt the music. If he felt a certain soloist should perform, they would be called off the cuff. He would test the crowd. If that performer could move the crowd, he might incorporate that solo into the show. He would experiment. Sometimes things worked and sometimes they didn't. He was constantly improving the show.

He played the keyboards and the drums. He actually played the drums on one of his best-selling hits. The story behind the scene is that we were in the studio ready to cut the song, and the drummer said,

"I need to go to the bathroom."

He ran out of the studio. You could never do that to Brown. James Brown sat on the drum kit and counted it off. Amazingly, that was the song he released and, like most of his songs at the time, it was a hit. He wasn't a great drummer, but he could get by just fine. He was good on the keyboard as well.

Mr. Brown was always striving to do something different. It wasn't that he was bored with his own songs – it was more than that. He always wanted to improve. It was difficult to have the musical ability Mr. Brown needed, and be able to transfer that ability so Brown could express in music what was in his head. He would throw out new ideas in a show, or in a rehearsal. We thought he was crazy.

138

Shockingly, half the time it would work! He came up with things that nobody had ever thought of before and it worked. It became "the thing."

Consider the raised-nine chord. It was a jazz chord. It was always leading to the next chord. He took that nine chord and made songs out of that; out of that ONE chord. It was amazing! He is famous for the one chord groove. The band fought him tooth and nail when he brought that idea out. They all thought he was wrong. He asked them,

"How does it sound?"

The band responded, "It sounds fine."

There you have it. He laughed; he knew. He did not care if music theory said he was wrong.

Understandably, he didn't know if music theory agreed with the ideas in his mind. He had no idea. He was creating new music theory. He simply heard and felt the music in his head. More often than not, it was brilliant.

Unfortunately, I was a part of the famous Sacramento trip. We were playing on Thanksgiving. Very few tickets were sold. Almost no one showed up. Mr. Brown simply left us - no gas for the bus, no money. That was the time we all quit. Most of the band stayed quit for several months, but not surprisingly, they all started going back to James Brown over time. Naturally, the band got back together. Not me. That is when I quit for seven years.

After Mr. Brown got out of prison I knew he would be hotter than ever. Sure enough, he was. It wasn't just that he was hot; he asked me to come back. I could not say "no" to James Brown.

I stayed with Brown because the music was interesting. It was great work and I got to see the world. I got paid well…when I got paid. The last 10 or 12 years were just great. The first 10 or 12 years were not so great. There were so many ups and downs. We were stranded at times. If he didn't get paid…we didn't get paid. It was as simple as that.

Mr. Brown was a private person. He was not the kind of guy that would tell you what he was thinking. He would rarely share private thoughts with you. The band was kept out of those conversations. He wanted to be in control of the band; total control. He would never let you know that he had any weakness. He always had to be on top. Total control was his thing even if he wasn't in total control of his own life. He always had to act like as if he was. It was hard to get close to him. It was hard to get him to open up. Every once in a while he would tell you a story about something that had happened to him. It was not a common occurrence at all.

During the last few months of his life he would come to the stage in a wheelchair. I saw it. If you want to understand James Brown, you have to understand: he had "pure will." That is why he was so successful. From the very beginning he would say,

"I am going to do this."

140

Whatever it would take, he would do. Nobody could tell him no. It was impossible. Record producers could not tell him no. They tried to tell him he could not record a live album. They were wrong. He proved them wrong. He paid for it himself, and" Live at the Apollo" became one of the greatest records of all time.

I was a white man in a black man's world. That made absolutely no difference to Mr. Brown. None at all! It didn't matter that I was a white trumpet player. I was "his" trumpet player. That's the way he looked at it. I didn't get any special privileges.

Eventually, he made me the band leader. He knew that I could handle it. I could do music. I could do arrangements. I could do whatever he asked. He saw that. I didn't ask for it, I didn't want it. I didn't want animosity from other players in the band. Some of them had been there longer than I had. Some may have been resentful. I was never ostracized by the band. We got along well.

Getting along with the band was like any other group of people that you work with. Some you liked quite well – others, not so much.

On the road we would pass the time by simply riding on the bus. There was so much bus riding. We drove coast-to-coast. We traveled from New York City to Vancouver. The trip took three days. We did two shows in New York and then traveled three days nonstop to Vancouver. We walked right onto the stage in Vancouver and performed two consecutive shows that night. It was unbelievable. We really were a funky band. It was four straight days without a shower. It was awesome!

We did our own thing. We had fun on the bus, played cards and backgammon, listened to music and maybe had a few drinks. I can't remember!

The world may never understand how much of a determined man James Brown really was. He was the most determined man that I have ever seen. I have never met anyone like him. He was a strong-willed man who came from abject poverty and turned himself into a world figure. He was known internationally better than any other man in the world. He was more famous than Muhammad Ali.

When you consider that he began his life dead (he was stillborn). They laid him over to the side while they worked with his mother. His aunt showed up shortly, blew into his nose and gave him life. He came from a very inauspicious beginning. That story always gets me. I can't imagine starting life that way.

He would never publicly talk about growing up in Georgia. He would never talk about being abandoned. He would never talk about growing up in a whorehouse. That is where his deep-seeded pain came from. That is the source of some of his animosity. It was a rough beginning for him, and this man took it and turned it into a career.

Performing helped him to get out of prison. He would sing in the prison. His friend Bobby Byrd got him out.

Bobby even let Mr. Brown live with him for a while. That is an overwhelming beginning to overcome. It is incredible. It always blows my mind to think about it.

You need to understand the song, "Please, Please, Please." It was a plea to the world. He was asking them not to leave. He must've sung that song a million times. Yet, it always sounded as though it was sung for the very first time. He would put his heart and soul into that song. He would let the audience have it.

The cape came from wrestler Gorgeous George. All of the capes, crowns, and jewels came from Gorgeous George. He would take his inspiration from a lot of people. Only some were musicians. He was a man who wanted a real show. He wanted to entertain the people. He would drop to one knee. People would start to help him up and walk with him offstage. As he neared the end, he would throw off the cape and run back to perform for the crowd. I suppose the first time someone threw a coat around him he liked it. It may have given him the idea. Let's try a cape!

I was on stage with James Brown when he performed with Michael Jackson at the BET (Black Entertainment Television) awards. We had no idea anything was going to happen. The plan was to present James Brown with a lifetime achievement award. They gave the award to Michael Jackson to present to Mr. Brown. Everybody went crazy. Michael and James started singing and dancing. That was it. End of story. Everybody loved it.

Remember, Michael Jackson got his moves from James Brown. He studied Brown religiously. He copied James Brown's moves. It was awesome. Then Brown placed his cape on Michael! The torch had been passed.

A couple of years before that event, we were performing in Beverly Hills. Michael Jackson joined us on stage. BB King was our opening act! Prince also came out and played guitar. Prince loved Mr. Brown. That's where he got a lot of his moves. That night was absolutely spectacular. We performed one show with four of the greatest entertainers of all time on stage. It was unbelievable!

As far as the show is concerned, I had nothing to do with the dancers or the backup singers. He even choreographed some of the dancers' and singers' moves. That was all him. I took care of the horns and the rhythm section.

I loved playing for the audiences. When I first began with Mr. Brown, it was primarily for black audiences. They seemed to accept me even though I couldn't dance. I had to learn how to dance. It was self-defense. I now have my moves down. I became a funky old white boy. After three or four years, the audience became mostly white. Toward the end it was 95% white. I suppose that was because he saturated the market between 1956 and 1974. "Earth, Wind and Fire" and various bands like them entered the market. His audience changed from mostly black to mostly white.

We performed thousands of times together. There are a few performances that stand out to me. Naturally, the experience in Soviet Georgia will always be with me. There was also a time that we sang in São Paulo, Brazil. The place was rocking! The bleachers were shaking. The stage was shaking. The entire stadium was moving. They started throwing coke bottles on stage from the upper balconies. We thought we were going to be killed. It got dangerous. Brown actually stopped the show. I had never seen him stop the show before. He simply stopped until the crowd calmed down.

We played Woodstock II in 1999. We played at the Kremlin - that was awesome. We actually played there twice. The last time was around the year 2000. Just before that show we were in Beirut, Lebanon. Some of the band refused to go. Beirut was sketchy then. We played Beirut and the Kremlin all in the same tour. Rarely has that happened in the history of the world.

They loved James Brown in Moscow. We actually played another time in Moscow as well. It was for a private party; James Brown and Jennifer Lopez (J Lo) performed. We played for a Russian tycoon. Some of those Russians have serious money. Brown was paid $300,000 for the show and I think J Lo was paid more because, at the time, she was really hot on the charts. All of the expenses, plane tickets, hotels, etc. were all paid by the Russian tycoon. It must've been more than $1 million just for his birthday party. I don't know his name - all I know is that he was a Russian tycoon. We didn't play together with J Lo. We began the show and when we were finished we packed up our instruments and left. It was kind of weird.

I will never forget the first show I ever did with James Brown. It was in Mexico City, Mexico. He was wearing a white jumpsuit. He did a couple of knee drops and I looked over and all I could see were bloodstains on his knees. Blood was soaking through his pants! I thought to myself, "Man - oh man - this guy is something! He makes his knees bleed every show!

He was also a giving man. He was giving on stage. Regardless, if he felt terrible or not, he would give everything to the audience. He would do knee drops when he could barely walk. His knees were arthritic. He did the splits a year or two before he died. I couldn't believe it. It was as though he got caught up in the moment and tried to give the audience everything he had. That is just the way he was. He would give it his all. He didn't care. It didn't matter if there were 50,000 people watching him perform or 50. I'm not exaggerating. He always performed with the utmost intensity. I remember playing three hours one night for 50 people. That is the way it was. He could've played 30 minutes and then left but that is not who James Brown was.

He did a lot of amazing things. When his father died, I went to the funeral. I went to Adrienne's as well. When my

146

father died, amazingly, he came to my father's funeral. He flew from Georgia to Nashville on a chartered jet, rented a limousine, and came to my house. He had met my father a few times. He told me what a good man he was. He had picked up that my father was a strict disciplinarian. He liked that. He appreciated that. He knew that is where I came from. He had such a good side. He shook my hand, and put his arm around me. That was how he expressed sympathy. I was grateful that he cared.

I remember playing a concert in Rio de Janeiro. He was so sick that the doctor had to come and put a catheter in him to receive antibiotics and fluids intravenously. He was really sick. When it came time for the show, he pulled the catheter out and went to perform the show. He performed for more than two hours. When the show was over, he went back to the hotel and had the catheter put back in. Can you imagine? The amazing thing about James Brown is he would go out the very next night and perform again.

It is important to understand - when James Brown was on the road he would get healthy. When he got home, he would get unhealthy. Do you know what I mean? After his performance in Croatia we had almost two months off. That is way too long for James Brown to be home. He could not come back from such a long stay at home. He would go home and not eat right. He would take too many drugs. His wife was not there to take care of him. He didn't have

147

people close to him to take care of him. In previous years we had always been able to save him. We would get him out on the road and get him right - get him healthy. His reason for living returned. He became excited again. He had things to do.

Even though he had done a million shows in his life, he would get excited about performing again. He loved it. He lived to perform for people. He had no hobbies. He did not play chess, he didn't golf, he didn't fish, and he didn't swim. Nothing. Zero. This, performing, was all he knew. That is sad.

James Brown's son joined the band toward the end. He did not receive any special treatment. That is not how James Brown would do things. He may have even been harder on Daryl than other members of the band.

He had a daughter that was always in trouble. Venisha Brown was arrested for drug use. She could imitate him to a "T." She could do the splits, sing like him, and perform like him. She was terrific. Unfortunately, she just couldn't stay out of trouble. They even did a show or two with her doing a tribute to her father with some of the band, but she couldn't stay out of trouble and that tribute show fell apart.

Of all the stars that we performed with, Michael Jackson was the most memorable. He was very nice. He was very friendly; Prince, not so much.

We performed with Donna Summer and George Benson sitting with us. That was terrific. We played with the Red Hot Chili peppers in London in front of 80,000 people. He didn't mind not being the top act when the money was right. We played in Mexico City with Jerry Lee Lewis. He said that he would open the show and let Jerry Lee close it. Normally, he would never do that. We performed with Chuck Berry in Japan and Brown went on first. He just wanted to get the show over with and get back to the hotel.

A few years earlier, he was supposed to open for the Rolling Stones in Madison Square Garden, but decided he did not want to open for them. He canceled the day of the show! This was back in the 1970s. He thought he was on top of the world. That upset me and everyone else in the band. We really wanted to play with the Rolling Stones. That is who he was. He didn't care. He would cut off his nose to spite his face. He would throw away thousands of dollars just to make a statement.

***

George "Spike" Nealy II

I'm your average bear.

There are so many more guys playing in this James Brown Band. You know nobody ever took notice of us. We're the reindeers that pull Santa's sleigh. We make Christmas happen every year, for everybody, but nobody really recognizes the reindeers.

I came to the James Brown Band in 1991. It was directly after he was released from prison. I was with the SOS

Band; I came along with James Brown Band right after that. It was one of those things; I was in the wrong place but I was at the right time when I got hired for the job. Pretty much everybody was hired that way, because he didn't do auditions. That was one of his things: he never did auditions. So, if you're playing for James Brown, if you're in the band, it's a strange way you got the gig. But it definitely wasn't through an audition. However, let me be clear: he always made sure your performance was superb. If not, you were gone. In that sense, we were auditioning every day.

Everything was spontaneous. James Brown could change things up spinning on a dime. We could pull up to the venue, go on stage for a concert, and you would not know exactly what you were going to play. That is one thing. Going on a TV show where the camera man or producers don't know what you're going to play is quite another. You always had to have your guard up. That's why it was almost like going to J B University. You had to be a scholar at knowing 6000 songs. Because out of 6000 songs, he could do any of the songs he wished. He had the confidence in his band that they would not miss the downbeat on any song.

It's not a 1, 2, 3, 4, play; it's a drop the hand, and it's full band! No time did we miss! As many times as we did Arsenio Hall, Johnny Carson, Keenan Ivory Wayans, Rosie O' Donnel Show, including CBS Morning, Good Morning

America, The Breakfast Show…we had to stay on top of our game. You can't just be on stage with James Brown. The main thing is you have to learn the man. You have to learn James Brown first. Then, after you understand James Brown, the music part becomes a little easier; but you have to understand him first.

What I'm talking about is how he feels his music. Music comes first. If anything was bothering you, if you have any kind of problems and let them get in the way (of performing), causing a mental block - he wanted that solved right away. Whether it's a bill you owe or you need to take care of, or something that's at home, Mr. Brown wanted to make sure that problem was taken care of. He needed our minds to be focused 100% on him. That focus is what he got from each of us. That's what made his band so special, and unique.

When we traveled to different music festivals, or when we would travel overseas, we would watch different bands perform on stage. They had music lists, music stands, show and song lists. It was all very orderly. When we come out, we are ready to hit - we are just waiting on the down beat.

They would ask us: "Hey man, what you guys gonna play tonight?"

"Well, your guess is good as mine. We don't have a clue, but I guarantee Mr. Brown has it in his head, once he starts to sing."

It isn't necessarily in his head before he sings. Once he starts to sing, he is going to give you a good show. In his mind, he understands that no two towns brought about the same vibe. They were different people in every town and so each performance had to be different.

"Sex Machine" might not be played in certain towns. We might never perform "Sex Machine" in Rome due to his respect for the Pope, even though the song doesn't mean anything sexual. It was simply out of respect for the Church.

He was very thoughtful about respecting different customs from different countries. He knew all of the uniforms that we had. He was a master at knowing what colors to wear, what colors to mix together, particularly when you are performing in these different countries. He was mindful of what colors not to wear when you are performing in a specific country or region. He wanted the person's mind solely latched or focused on him when you watched the performance on stage. He wanted you to get so deeply involved in what was taking place that you left that venue completely satisfied.

I enjoyed every minute of it and I really miss him. I think everybody in the band misses him - for the little things he would say and the lessons that he taught off stage, more so than the music on stage. The people he played for, his audience - they miss the music and the man onstage. We miss the man.

He was definitely a teacher about the things in life. Down here at the University, South Carolina State University, I pull a lot from James Brown (Spike now directs the Marching Band). I want to keep these guys sharp. A lot of times they don't understand where I am coming from. I incorporate how Mr. Brown would teach different things about performing. When you see this band, you understand why the pants on the band members are the same level. You understand why everything is cut sharp and neat. That is the way James Brown wanted his band to appear on stage.

In the summertime, we have pre-drill in August. I make sure these guys are well drilled. I want them to know what they should expect and be prepared for anything. I want them to stay on top of their game and stay on top of their music. I want them to stay on top of their "look." I want them to be aware of the visual elements of performing, as well as the audio portion. I want a deaf person to watch the show and enjoy it visually. I want a blind person to enjoy the audio portion of the show. You have to be able to entertain for the deaf as well as the blind, and I always share that with them.

There was never a night when we went on stage with Mr. Brown that each wrinkle wasn't a $25 fine. Whatever it touched was an additional $25 for connecting to that wrinkle. Your shoes had to be shined. You had to be shaved and neatly groomed. That is the way we would travel. That is the way the stage was set. He wanted his audience to get a nice picture. He wanted his audience to be completely relaxed when they sat back. He wanted you to enjoy the show.

We wondered sometimes why we had to travel with ties on and dressed in suits. All of that wondering stopped when we flew to the Netherlands and we performed in the North Sea Jazz Festival. When we arrived, we went directly to the North Sea Jazz Festival; straight to the venue. Once we got to the venue it was show time. The luggage was left at the departure airport. It was a weight issue with the airplane and the uniforms were left behind. I think they remained in Italy. They were going to arrive after the performance. People who saw the show thought that was our uniforms - but those were our traveling clothes; shirts and tie. From that experience alone, we understood why he had us travel ready to do our thing.

Once we landed, the cameras followed him. Because we dressed so neatly there was never a bad shot of the entourage or a bad shot of the band. We never wanted to do anything that would compromise the image of James Brown.

I miss him; I just miss him, so much.

I'm a person that if I want to know something, I ask. I'm not going to be stand-off-ish. He and I would have this thing. After every show, he would give me a call in the room and ask me, "Nealy, what did you think about the show tonight?"

I don't hold back the truth. I would tell him exactly what I thought about the show. I'd say, "Mr. Brown, the show was okay."

But then I would tell him about certain things that needed to be addressed. He'd say, "You didn't think I was going to remember…"(the thing that I was talking about). Of course, I knew he would remember every moment of the show.

I responded, "Yes sir Mr. Brown. I figured you weren't going to forget."

He would ask me every night what I think about the show, and each night I would tell him, because each night was full of amazement for me. Even though I had been in the band all those years, it was an amazing thing for me to watch him. To see the show and see a show of a man of that age, who could just keep poppin' and poppin' with that energy.

I remember we went on stage, then off stage. We boarded a private jet and flew to another country. We did a show and then ran back to the airport. The plane took off and we ate dinner up in the air. The plane landed and we were off to another show. We left that show, ran back to the runway, traveled by bus back to the hotel for two hours of sleep. We then boarded a private plane to do another show! It makes you tired just thinking about it – but not James Brown. He had a different motor.

Man, after we finished doing that about twelve times we were exhausted. We had nothing left. It reminded me of our last run. It was so heavy back in 2006. We had done so many gigs in a row, and we were up in the Northern end of Europe and in Russia. We were in the Balkans, and every performance we were just pumping, pumping, pumping. Everyone was so drained.

One night he smiled and said, "Get in there, I'm 70 years old, let's go!"

You looked up and said, OH MY GOODNESS! How does he do it?

Each person in the show would reach down and pull some of that magical energy out. You had to do it for The Man.

Another part that was amazing for me was he didn't use pencil or paper. He had a memory, man. He had a memory like an elephant. He had a photographic memory. He could remember any kind of numbers: telephone numbers, overseas numbers, dates, and places. He was a genius at remembering things like that. He could quote Bible verses or paraphrase different scriptures out of the Bible. He was a genius at knowing things from the Bible, front to back.

Whenever we were in the United States and we had a show on Saturday night, no matter where we were in the

States, he was back on the private jet to attend church Sunday morning. We were still on the road, but he was back in church Sunday morning, and then he would fly to join us.

When he would fly the band down for rehearsal in Augusta for two weeks, we were his family. We were his family and he enjoyed being around and with us. He told me one time,

"Mr. Nealy, as long as I am out on the road, I am always James Brown. Once I go behind my gates on the estate, I am regular granddaddy."

When we were in Belgium, we had one night where a group of blind kids came to the show. Mr. Brown was very good to the blind kids. They couldn't see the show, but they could "feel" the show. Everything had to be sharp musically. Everything like clapping your hands, the crowd participation, everything had to stand out so even though they couldn't see him visually, they could see him in their minds.

The next night he had the group of deaf kids come to the show – and the same principle applied. They couldn't hear it, but they could see it. He made the sound technicians turn up the base for the entire show. He wanted the kids to "feel the vibe, feel the 'thump."

It was amazing to watch and witness this man. He was a man that was so ahead of time at making things happen, no matter the challenge.

I wasn't the only one he talked to after the show. There was another guy down in his dressing room - Robert "Mousey" Thompson from Washington, D.C. Sometimes we sat in his room and ate ice cream and talked about the show. We would be listening to a playback of the show.

Brown would say, "Order anything you want, order ice cream."

We would sit there, relax and listen to the whole show.

After we finished the show, we would talk a little bit. I remember one time he said,

"Mr. Nealy, we goin' to Russia."

That was at a time in history when you could forget about traveling to Russia - it was still the USSR. The curtain was still up. He said,

"Mr. Nealy, we are going to Russia, and we going behind the curtain son."

I said, "Wow, Mr. Brown. You mean in Russia behind the curtain?"

"Yes," he said, "Russia, behind the curtain."

I tell you, it was no less than three or four years, the next thing you know, passports were turned in, visas and everything came through, and we were on stage, at the Kremlin. That blew - my - mind! There were guards still on duty. That was a magical moment.

Another magical moment is when we performed in Serbia and Bosnia when that war was going on. The United Nations called for a 48 hour cease fire. People on both sides stopped fighting for 48 hours. We were playing at the Coliseum, everybody came to the show, and everybody had a ball! The white UN tanks surrounded the Coliseum during the entire show. Immediately after the show we went to the hotel. We had an early check-out that morning. We flew out with no problem at all. That was an amazing thing to see.

There is something about his music. The fire he brought to this turmoil. We would always watch CNN. I watched the news and heard about turmoil somewhere in the world. I would call my momma and say, "Momma, we are going. Because wherever trouble is James Brown is going to go. He figures whatever the trouble is he could soothe that thing out."

When we performed in Lebanon during a military action; it was amazing. Right before the show a tank traveled through the downtown. It went right through the middle of the street, passed our hotel and the ground was shaking. It was a tank! Not a car, not a Volkswagen, but a full tank! It went past our street right before the concert. We did not have one problem!

It's those times that I remember him most. You just knew you were not performing for an ordinary man. He had to have some kind of special thing on him.

Mr. Brown had two of everything. However, before he went to two drummers he had three drummers. The thing people need to understand, is he needed "fresh feet" all the time. If it's a two hour show, you need that fresh driving beat for two hours. If it is a three hour show, you need that fresh driving beat for three hours. At no time, should that beat change or fall short. He definitely insisted on a HEAVY one. And ONE puts it all together.

As a drummer you can get lost and always come back to the ONE. The band could get lost and find their way back, because the drummer is always going to be HEAVY on the ONE.

We had two drummers. Many people thought both drummers played at the same time. That was not true. Each drummer had their own of series of songs that Mr. Brown was comfortable with. He would only point and turn it back over to the other drummer to change out if he needed a fresh beat on top. Then he would simply turn and point to another drummer.

Mr. Brown would often go off script. That is why we didn't have a show or a song list. The band looked at him as the authority to change anything.

Number one rule for the band was no towels on the stage. No water on the stage. That was difficult. Certain members of the band threw off a lot of sweat yet we could not put a towel on the stage.

I asked the stage manager, Mr. Tompkins, about the towel. He said, "If you use a towel, when you wipe your sweat, by the time you get through wiping, you have missed something…you missed something."

160

I understood perfectly well what he was saying. I knew we were getting ready to get to the end of the song and I had just a few measures to get to the end. I was squeezing that eye. One eye was already closed, holding the sweat back. I'm squeezing that eye and I only have two. I would say to myself, "Just a little bit more. Just a little bit more and this song will be over." And then...I get a chance to just real quick, wipe, just wipe this eye real quick.

By the time I got done doing that little half-second wipe, we're down to the end of the song. His three fingers are up in the air. Now, I don't know exactly what he has done. Did he do the three fingers down by his side first or did he just hold the three fingers up?

A lot of our shows are done by signals, like baseball players. I don't know if he went down first or up? The three fingers already up - so now I'm stuck. If he went down first, we are already done. If not, he is going for the solo. Oh man, I got about three seconds to figure this thing out. I got to do "eeny, meeny, miney, moe", in my head. Which one is it? Ohhhhh boy!

Okay, of course, I chose the wrong one! The band cuts off and I'm still playing. I'm still playing and he looks up at me. This is James Brown, he didn't panic. Not a problem. If you want a solo, you got it. The whole band left the stage. I am standing up there by myself! I'm playing the congas; playing a solo. He finally brought the band back on after about a good ten minute solo. He brought seventeen, eighteen people back - one by one!

Listen, by the time everyone was back I am down to one knee. The audience thought it was part of the show. Everybody was clapping. I was down to one knee. My fingers were bleeding. By the time he brings everybody back on stage, I was trying to hit the last note. He said,

"Ladies and gentlemen, give a big round of applause, Mr. Nealy, give a big round of applause."

From that point on, I made sure: do not put a towel over by me. I got taught that lesson. That was my lesson right there.

He could tell if something was not just right. He had a great ear. He would call you in after the show. For example, he would hear the guitar player hit a wrong note or make the wrong chord. He would remember the exact chord even though you might not remember. Sometimes, you hit that note, you know you hit it, but you thought you hid it from him. No chance! This was James Brown. He would call you in and tell you what note you hit or what part of the song or what chord you missed. At no time could you miss a chord or not play the note out. He would call out a chord and expect you to hit it. He knew the note you needed to play before you did.

I remember one night during that same run. We were flying, staged, back to the hotel, back to the private plane, back to the hotel, flying everywhere. We were out performing shows about thirteen times. I was exhausted! When we boarded the plane I peeked up toward the front. Where he was sitting. I thought I saw him fast asleep. This seemed like a good time to get a nap in. I dozed off. I got a little nap in.

While I am sleeping I could feel somebody on the side of me. I cracked one eye, real slowly. When I cracked that eye, Mr. Brown was staring me dead in my face. He's kneeled down in the aisle, I cleared my throat and apologetically said, "Mr. Brown, uh, how you doing Mr. Brown?" He said, "I'm alright. Son, I tell you, what you been doing with your nights, Mr. Nealy? You look a little tired!"

"Golllly!" It was one of those moments. You are trying to figure him out. What do you think I have been doing with my nights?

I can't tell you how amazed we were at the energy of Mr. Brown. He was now past the 70 mark. At age 72 he was still full speed ahead.

Negative sells regarding James Brown. It doesn't surprise me. It doesn't surprise me at all. But if you are going to be fair about it you have to talk about everything good, too. By the time you finish talking about everything good, that bad is nothing more than a drop of water in a bucket. When you weigh the good and the bad of James Brown, I can't find the bad.

Everything that I have been talking about is pretty much on the good side. That's not done intentionally. It is just the way it was. I didn't have to figure out what I should say. I'm just telling about my days with the band and Mr. James Brown.

I'm a person that loves kids. I love them every day. I tried to have at least 13 or 15 kids at the show. Sometimes I would need to go to a child center before the show and invite some kids. I always tried to get them backstage. Mr. Brown would always take pictures with all the kids I would bring backstage. He would sing whatever things they wanted, as long as it was for the kids.

I had performed with many artists that were cutting tracks the "new school way." With percussion, I'd be the last one going in the studio. If I wanted to put a tambourine on top of the track, I would go and put the tambourine in. Sometimes I would go back in and put in the cabasa. You have so many tracks to add on top.

With James Brown, when I first went in the studio, he did it the "old style." Everybody is in the studio at the same time. The last recording he did is called "Gut Bucket Funk." Horns were with open microphones, as was everyone. When I or anyone else hit something hard, you can't erase it. Everybody in the studio is going to pick it up. There are no ways to erase it off the track.

I learned real quick, if Mr. Brown is recording and he gets his part right, and 9 times out of 10 he will, he is not going to go back in and change it. If you made a mistake, that mistake is now on the CD. He will not change it. Every time, every take, you make sure you give it your all, don't take it lightly.

If he said, "Okay, gentlemen, we are just going to rehearse this one time…" Don't fall for that.

Because when you go through it the one time, it is being recorded and he would say, "Gentlemen, have a nice day, I see you tomorrow."

It's over with. We have finished recording.

I asked him the first time we had finished recording everything.

I said, "Mr. Brown, you want me to go back in and put a cabasa (or some other instrument) on top of that?"

He said, "What you want to go mess with something God did?"

"I said, yes sir, I understand." He said, "Son, have a nice day. See you tomorrow."

He would always tell me, "First time, first time is God. Second time, that's you messing with what God gave you and put in your mind to do." So, we never did a second take.

When you were recording with James Brown it was just one take. We would not stay in the studio all day trying to get a track right. It was one take for us. We were in there and then quickly out of there.

"Cut the check," we're through.

James Brown was a musical genius. There is absolutely no doubt about that. If you would show him a chord on paper he could not tell you what the chord was. But if you tell him to spell the chord, he'd spell it right out to you, and that's any chord you might name. If you tell him to spell the diminished chord and asked, "What was the third?" He has got you beat.

If you thought he didn't know what he was talking about, you just had to wait until after the show.

He would say, "You thought I didn't know what I was talking about when I tell you I want a flat 9. I want a flat 9!"

Right along with having a photographic memory, he knew the chords and the chord progressions. People study for a lifetime what just came naturally for him. He was a genius - and it was combined with God's gift. His understanding of music was just something that was gifted to him.

When I first began with the band, we were playing up in San Francisco. It was in The Round. The Round is where the stage rotates in a circle. Usually it is just the headline act that is on the round. This time, Mr. Brown put the entire band on the rotating stage with him. Everybody is making a twirl.

The light goes down, and then off, and just as I am ready to hit the drums I see the security guy bring Mr.

Brown's wife over toward me. He places her in the chair right over in my percussion rig – right where I am sitting.

As I'm getting ready to hit this roll I'm telling him, "Hey, she can't sit there! Don't put her there."

I don't have control of the environment. If the stick breaks it could fly off and hurt her. A stick breaks every night. You have no idea where it's going to land. If it hurts me, okay - it's fine. But I didn't want to harm her in any way.

It was too late. Drum roll started the show. Every now and then I would glance back to see if she was okay. Now I was distracted. My job was to keep my mind on her husband, Mr. Brown. I didn't want him to think badly of me - but I can't watch her anymore. This is my gig. I need to watch Mr. Brown. He's calling out songs, and reaching for multiple instruments.

After the show was over, we received a big standing ovation. Everyone was clapping for Mr. James Brown. Mr. Brown exited the stage and the band hit the last note. We took the last bow and the lights come up. I looked around and saw Mrs. Brown's hair done like the chickens done got in it. It had nothing but sawdust; little chips of wood all through her hair.

Aw….man!! This is not good. I didn't want to say anything because I know that she hasn't looked in the mirror yet.

I said, "Mrs. Brown, Mrs. Brown, I am so sorry that any wood from the sticks got in your hair."

She replied, "Oh, no problem no problem Mr. Nealy."

I said to myself, "I know she is saying no problem now, but wait until she gets to that dressing room and looks in that mirror. Oh man, I have got to get to that dressing room. I'm getting my clothes on real fast. I know they are going to be calling for me."

I get my clothes on and someone knocks on the door saying, "Mr. Nealy, Mr. Brown wants to speak to you."

Oh boy, here we go. I walked down to the dressing room and say "Mr. Brown, its Mr. Nealy."

"Come on in son." I went on in.

Mrs. Brown had two other people helping her pick wood out of her hair. As I'm standing there I thought, "Well, it was fun while it lasted. I know I am fired."

I said, "Mrs. Brown, let me apologize to you, before you say anything. Let me just apologize. When the gentleman put you in the kit, in the percussion kit, where I was performing, I knew it was going to be a problem. I tried to tell him before the show started that it was going to be a problem…"

Mr. Browns interrupted me and said, "Mr. Nealy, the reason I called you in here, is not because of my wife's hair. My wife asked me to call you in here because my wife asked me how much money you are making. She didn't know whether to watch you, or watch me. She was having

168

such a great time sitting back watching you play. So, how much money you making?"

I told him that I was just coming on. I was making $450 a week.

He said, "Son, you are now making $550 a week. Son, you don't have to be with me a long time, but I will make you a wealthy man."

Every week he called me into the dressing room and said, "Son, how much are you making?"

I said, "$550 a week."

He said, "Now you making $650.

The Man kept his word. You didn't have to be with him for a lifetime. He would teach you the art of entertaining; to find the borderline that entertains all colors, races, creeds, everyone.

***

Robert "Mousey" Thompson

A friend called me up one day and asked "Hey, you want to be with Mr. Brown and do it with James Brown?" At this point in my career I thought it would be a hit and miss kind of situation.

I ended up spending 13 years with the man.

I traveled to Augusta. My friend had made it seem as though I had the job before I got there. It did work out that way, but I had to audition. There were drum sets and drummers everywhere auditioning for this job.

To make a long story short, we rotated, and he brought me back to the drum kit 2 or 3 times. When he finally made his decision, he told me to sit right there at the drum kit. He thanked everybody for coming.

He looked at me and said, "Welcome to the family son."

I was with him til the end.

Daryl Brown did not audition with me at that time. But even Daryl would not have a chance. You've got to realize now, that when I went after this job I was real hungry. You know, you can't mess with a hungry man when it comes to going after a job. The hungry individual is always going to get it, definitely.

He wanted us to be polished, and in uniform. He wanted us to wear suits. After traveling on the bus thousands of miles he wanted you still in a suit and tie. He wanted us to look sharp. He knew if the band looked sharp, it would be a positive reflection on him. People would always compliment us on our dress.

We weren't able to wear jeans or sneakers or things like that. That was forbidden. It was almost like the military. If you were used to taking orders, nothing would bother you.

He treated me like his own son. Daryl would probably tell you himself that he actually treated me better than his own son. He was real tough on Daryl.

James Brown would talk to me often. He would call me up in the middle of the night. It didn't matter with Mr. Brown. It was an honor just to be affiliated with him. In the beginning, I was just like a fan. Over time, I became like a family member. The difficult times would just blow out the window - just as a normal family.

He could call to talk about the show.

"What do you think about the show son?"

It was 4 o'clock in the morning! And so you would be up talking about that show. You would only talk about the good parts. You didn't want to bring anything up that wasn't straight.

It was important we represented Mr. Brown well. We wanted to be a great band. But it wasn't as though we were trying to be a superstar that was working with a Mega-Star. Working with him put us in a position to be stars.

When I joined Mr. Brown he said, "Hey your life is going to change completely now."

I listened to him, but I didn't really listen. Today people approach me and say, "You're a legend man; you a legend." I don't believe what they are saying.

I tell them, "I'm simply doing God's work."

Working with James Brown gave me the opportunity to work with kids. I am able to teach them the same things he taught me. I try to put it in their gear. I try to teach them small lessons, such as keeping their uniform on or abiding by the rules.

He was a musical genius. He was phenomenal. He would talk to you about something that would happen in the future. I often thought, 'Yeah, yeah right, what is he talking about?' The next thing I knew. It was happening just like he said it would.

I remember when he came into rehearsal one day and said, "The record business is over as we know it."

He was talking about the internet and digital sales years, before we understood the reach of digital downloads, iTunes, etc. Ironically, he didn't even like computers.

Mr. Brown didn't talk about a specific religion. I can't say that he went every Sunday, but I know he was a godly person. He talked about love all of the time. He was such a loving person. Whatever demons he may have had, he always had a message of love and togetherness. Even in our shows he would always tell people "Look to your left tell the person sitting next to you, 'I love you.' Now look to your right and tell that person that you love them."

He was a man that could influence 100,000 people in the audience with his performance. That is nothing but God. He was a vessel of God's work. What happened with Brown in his private life was his business. Brown was Brown. We all have stories to tell about the bad in our own lives. For the most part, he was a good man.

There are superstars in the music industry. But James Brown was a man that played the game on an entirely differently level. He was a special gift to the world and people don't understand that.

What he did was amazing. For a man with a seventh grade education to go as far as he did in music and business, as well as stopping riots in '68 is unbelievable. Do you know people that can do that today? He was a man that could walk in and talk to presidents, kings, princes, and princesses, all around the world.

People think I'm a millionaire because I performed with James Brown. I'm not a millionaire, but I've sat at tables with millionaires working with Mr. Brown. To be around Brown, as loving and caring as he was, made me feel good. I felt like a millionaire. I felt like a million bucks when I was around Brown, period.

James Brown pulled me out of Southeast Washington D.C. and took me on an unbelievable journey. I have worked with other great artists like Peaches and Herb, Wilson Pickett, Rupert Thomas and Collin Thomas. They have all called me. But working with James Brown was special, beyond words. I thank God for that.
He left me as his number one drummer. Of course we had two drummers and we were up on stage together as friends. But I always felt special. Just like any football game, I wanted to be the quarter back. Even though he went through other drummers - I never left. Brown admired me and thanked me for that. He even apologized to me a few

times when something went wrong in the show. I was shocked - it was his show.

He would tell me, "Ah it's my fault, my bad, I'm sorry, I take that one."

Whatever conversation we had, he would take the lead. If you had an idea - it became his idea. If you were smart - you would let him have it. We talked about opening restaurants together. I still want to open a James Brown soul city café. I approached him with theme restaurants - we were never able to get them off the ground. I wanted the food named after his songs. Imagine "I Feel Good" Chicken Wings.

James Brown was just an amazing chap. Any time you had with the man was valuable time. I would ride with him on the private jet. He would keep me up all night talking about the show, telling stories, and make us all laugh. By the time we were getting ready to land, he would take a big yawn and say, "Aw, you better get some sleep."

We had to go directly to the venue to do a sound check. He was concerned about the strength of our beat that night. We were weak; our foot was weak because we needed to sleep. James Brown may not have needed sleep but we did. I wanted to cuss him out but never could.

I loved the road. It hurt me to go home and to watch him always get involved in his mess. He loved being on the road. He was straight. The venues we played were in areas of the world I never expected to see; Prague, Russia,

Lebanon, Africa and the Orient. I felt like I was living history.

People all over the world liked his music because it is like Pharrell - it makes them happy. What most people don't understand is that songs would come to him spontaneously, "in his space." I wanted the world to see "that space" and appreciate how kind and caring the man really was. He was not a cruel person - he just wanted to get the job done.

I'm quite sure that everybody knows by now he was a Republican at heart, but I'm not sure. He was really about supporting good men. He loved the presidents - all of them. He loved Strom Thurmond and Lindsey Graham. Some politicians wanted his endorsement - some did not. Regarding politics he would say, "I don't want a hand out, I want a way out." That was his big thing.

Brown was brilliant, but it was a little like college; sometimes you would have to decipher what was being said to break the code. He had a little glitchy thing in his voice. He was always adding soul and rhythm - salt and pepper - to his voice and to his music. It brings back fond memories when someone talks like him. Spike Nealy gets it the best.

James Brown taught me a very important lesson once. As you know, it was his way or the high way. One time he got me so fired up I was going to quit. I looked at him and I was mad. He knew I was furious. I put my drumsticks down on the floor tile - I was gone.

He said, "Son, whatever you do, don't fire yourself, let me fire you."

I had to think about that one. What did he mean by that? If I fired myself, I would never have a chance to come back. If he fired me, the door was always open because that was his call. I tell people that today.

While we were on the road, he was always working and calling critical people. I'm not denying that he didn't call his family members, but the band was closer to him than his family. We were with him on the road together, breaking bread, so close, like family. He always cared for us - he knew we loved him. Everybody in the band looked up to him like a father.

There would be times when I needed extra cash. I approached him.

"Mr. Brown I need...,"

He didn't let me complete my sentence. "What you needing son?"

He would give me the money but it would have some rap with it.

This is a great story of the kind of man James Brown was. I had on these shades (sunglasses) and he liked them. Remember, I had borrowed a nice sum of money from him.

He said, "Well I'm going to take 500 dollars out of your paycheck, you know, for you to pay that loan back."

I had no problem with that. 'Thank you, sir.'

176

I walked into this particular gig with his favorite pair of glasses. They had shaded lens like yellow or orange. We called them uppers. They were used for different kinds of light.

Mr. Brown walked up to me and said, "Man, those are sharp glasses you've got!"

I asked him if he liked them. I told him, "They're yours."

What he said was so funny.

"What, it's your shine? You can't give me your glasses!"

I think I paid 10 dollars for the glasses. I was happy to give them to him.

Remember, I owed him $500.

He later walked up to me and said, "When was the last time you had a raise?"

He was thinking about me - he really cared about his people.

I told him that it had been a year or so.

"Well I'm going to give you another raise." The raise was $500. He washed out the loan. As soon as the loan was paid, I was now making really good money. It started with a pair of $10.00 glasses. It started with a very gracious man. I will never work for another man like that.

There was a time when I needed $3,000.

I went to him and said, "Mr. Brown I need about $10,000."

I was bold. I sold it. He ended up giving me six or seven thousand dollars. I knew he wouldn't give me the entire amount - but I had a very important bill to pay and I knew that he cared enough to help me on a personal level.

He had a sense of humor about the women he was with. I don't know when he had time to do what he had to do behind closed doors. I don't know how many women he may have pulled in, but he would say to me grinning from ear to ear, "I did a nickel today."

Just think about a nickel, it's like he had five orgasms. I would say, "Yeah. Is that right?"

I would just listen and let it go in one ear and out the other - but he made me laugh. We really didn't have time for that. I wanted to get to bed as quickly as I could. I needed my sleep.

When I started with Brown I was a two-pack a day cigarette smoker. I needed to quit just so I could stay up with the man. He had us going at an unbelievable pace. I had to quit if I was going to carry this train.

You could not afford to be tired or lack focus. You had to watch the man closely. If you didn't, he would start flicking the hand, 5, 10, 15, 20. That five could have meant 100. You didn't know what the number was. Oh lord! I never asked what it was, because I always watched his signals. It was a precise machine.

Mr. Brown called me once. I was nervous, "Oh, oh, here we go." We were in Texas and Brown had just flown in from Washington D.C. I found out the other drummer had quit to become a preacher. His name was Arthur Dixon. I now had to carry the whole show by myself. That was the first time I had been trusted to carry the band.

Mr. Brown always wanted two musicians - he never wanted to have just one. I held my own during the show, but he still had another drummer flown out the following day. Our show was at least two hours - sometimes we went three. I had to be on - no room for mistakes. I was a great drummer, but I was playing for the best entertainer in the world. If you worked for Brown you had to be a "mean-some-body."

As I became more familiar with the show I would have little segues into certain songs. James Brown would let me play a little bit, and then he would call me out. I was that anxious quarterback that wanted to get out and run. I was like Washington Redskins quarterback RG3. I couldn't wait to get in and get after it.

After Dixon quit, Mr. Brown said, "Okay you're my number one drummer now."

He didn't curse. Believe it or not, he didn't curse around people. If he cursed, if he would say damn, in front of the ladies, he'd quickly say, "Excuse me ladies, I'm sorry." He was apologetic to all. If he got real pissed and a colorful word would come out his mouth he would apologize - especially if there were any ladies around.

With rap music he arrived to the point where he didn't want his music sampled. You need to understand this about the man.

He said, "If it's not a record that you can take home to mamma, then it shouldn't be played."

That makes sense. You don't want your mother listening to hoes and bitches - gangsters using the N word. No!

Look at what has happened since then. He was way ahead of his time. He saw the problems in music coming. He tried to put the rappers' minds right, but it seemed like the system just worked against him. That is why we are suffering now; violence and sexual exploitation. I have nothing against rap music, it can be prolific. But a lot of it can be damaging, and I think I have seen more of the damaging part. I look at the music the way it is today I'm like, 'Wow, where are we headed?'

I thank God for the music left behind from the people who have now passed on. It is nice to have some music we can still appreciate. As we get older that's all we have. I still listen to and record with some of the new artists. When I sit back and think about it, I'm not sure I want to be a part of this generation of music. I never had that problem with James Brown.

If a married woman was near him he was always respectful. When I was hired he didn't treat my wife with any disrespect or show disrespect to any woman. When you hear about things about he and his wife, you were only getting half of the story. I've never seen him hit a woman or anything like that. I'm just like any other person when I hear stories about Brown. 'Wow.' I'm in amazement, but that's his family life not mine.

James Brown was his own man. Look around, he had a private jet, he was an entrepreneur. Back in the 60s, c'mon you didn't meet a black man doing this. Everybody looked up to him. At the same time, there were people who started tearing him down later on in the 90s. He was the one who brought us: "I'm black and I'm proud." He gave us a culture we didn't have. We didn't recognize who we were. He made black people discover their humanity.

I'm proud because James Brown said that record was for everybody. You didn't need to be black. It was if you were down on your luck you could say, "I'm black but I'm proud…" He wanted to lift people - all people.

Of course, it was particularly important to black people - but it had to be. He came from an era where black people were not allowed to use the same bathroom or same water fountain.

When James Brown played with Pavarotti, it was chilling. All I can say is chilling, man. It brought tears to my eyes seeing him and Pavarotti sing Man's World. I knew it was a historical moment. These two great men together; who would have thought the Godfather of Soul, Mr. Please, Please, Please, the originator of Funk would have been

181

singing with one of the greatest tenor voices the world has ever known? Rap music could never achieve such heights. Pavarotti and James Brown - something like that will never be done again. It was ahead of its time. They could release that record today and even though both men are dead it would be #1.

That was a beautiful moment. People in the audience were in tears. I literally saw people crying – both men and women. That is how beautiful the song was. James Brown had the ability to move people. Once again, that's God's gift. I have watched people fall to their knees when they saw this man. A friend of mine from Senegal met Mr. Brown, and he immediately dropped to his knees and started crying. He never thought he would meet a man like that.

When we were in Japan I saw a tattoo of James Brown on one man's arm. This man is going to his grave with James Brown on his arm. That is heavy; it is phenomenal. I saw things just like that all over the world. Mr. Danny Ray would always say, "The world's Godfather of Soul, James Brown."

I rolled with him; I mean I had to ride in the car with him. We would drive into a gas station and a little kid would talk to Mr. Brown.

"What you doing son?"

"Oh I'm in school Mr. Brown."

He would then reach in his pocket and give the little boy money - sometimes big money - when he heard anything positive from the young man or woman. I saw him give out money so many times I lost track. Black, white, it didn't matter. He was a giving man. I don't care what they say about him, he was a giving man.

I don't ever see the news report on all of the good he did - just his mess. Of course, he gave away much of his money privately. That's sad; people give up their life to make us happy, and then we just throw darts to bring them down. I don't really want to see that kind of stuff. I would always defend the man because I knew the real James Brown.

I never did sense that we were not going to play together again or that he would die. He was a strong man. The night he died I was talking to Daryl. He called about 11 o'clock. James Brown was in the hospital with pneumonia. We were going to cancel the show the day after Christmas but we were still planning on New Year's.

I told Daryl, "When he gets out the hospital man, we're going to have to put our foot in his ass and make sure we get a cook out to his house."

We needed to get a nutritionist out there, somebody that was going to cook his meals and make sure he took his medication. The next call I received from Daryl was telling me that he is gone. I didn't understand.

"What do you mean he is gone?"

183

I thought he got up and left the hospital because that was the kind of man he was. He would say, "Hey, I'm not going to stay here, I'm out."

I was in denial. It still hadn't hit me. Finally, I was packing to go out on the road and started watching the news. I stopped packing and I just lost it from that point. My phone rang, rang, and rang. I had to unplug - I couldn't talk to everybody, it was so overwhelming.

Years have now gone by, and when I hit the stage and play his music, I still feel him there. It is eerie. I had the experience recently when I was in France. I felt as though Brown's presence was right there with us, you know, and the main thing we wanted to do was just keep his music and his legacy moving forward.

His faults were many, but they were his faults, not mine.

The last time we were in London playing, I began to notice he was losing a significant amount of weight. When the show was ending and he had the cape on and would walk away - he had nothing left to give. That was a great part of his act. This last time he exited the show he started to lean on the keyboards. He looked around at the band. Something moved me. I said to myself, 'No I've got to get him off the stage.' I took it upon myself. I walked him to the microphone, "Hey give it up for James Brown!" That was not my job - it was Danny Ray's - but I knew he was about ready to fall out. He had gotten small - real small.

***

Danny Ray – The Cape Man

My job was to keep everybody in check, tight. My job was to keep people clean. I was the Cape Man. I gave Mr. Brown the idea for the cape. The James Brown look was because of me. That's the only way you can do it.

People watch everything. The look was about details. From the moment people look at the stage, they are looking at everything, from head to toe. How you bring it, how you present it, it's all about the look. Either you are dedicated or you are not dedicated.

Mr. Brown and I would talk off stage, just before the show. I'd peek outside of the curtain. He would ask if the people out there were ready to go. The performance was the most important thing in our entire life. That would keep us going. It is that thought that you are trying to communicate. You must try to bring your best at all times. If you do it right, it pays off. It pays off. Everything in the show needed to be spot on. I believe in it that way, you know. Your appearance means a great deal.

Mr. Henry Stallings started doing his hair. As a matter of fact, we met in New York. He was from Augusta, Georgia. I met him in New York. That's where a lot of things started for me. The Apollo Theater - you know. Stallings would always see somebody worried about their appearance, and he would find them and get it right.

My job is to be on top of things. I needed to make sure I could find the guys. I needed to make sure their clothes were perfect, all the wrinkles were gone. I did a good job. Brown's manager, Tony Walker, knew I was doing a better job than the other man. He asked me if I wanted to work for Brown. I said, "Sure." He asked me to do the job. He wanted it done correct.

That is how I got to working with him. I watched the show a few times. There was a man named Luke from Macon, Georgia. He had a band and I watched it growing up. He gave me ideas.

Mr. Brown asked me, "Have you seen the show Mr. Ray? How many times?"

I told him that I had seen the show about, seven, eight, or nine times.

He said, "Tonight is your night!"

I looked at him like he was crazy.

"What are you talking about?"

We stepped in the dressing room together and I said, "Oh my God!"

He smiled and walked out.

We were up in Streets, Maryland. I went on stage and started saying: "Jaaaaaaaames Brown, James Brown, James Brown (alternating pitch and inflection)..." We were in a big arena. I said to myself, 'Lord, I can't back down now.' I was trying to think of everything I was supposed to do on the way to the stage. I think if somebody would've touched

186

me on the back of the legs I would have fallen down. I was so nervous.

The microphone got about that big (hands open wide). I had never heard myself on a microphone before, you know. That is a whole other thing to speak into a big mike and hear yourself. The first time was weird. I got through that night and I said to myself, "You got to do it, you got to do it."

Somebody said to me, "You'll get it - you got it man!" I was so nervous.

The problem was, he had that band behind you hittin' hard. It was 22 pieces of a big band hitting it hard. When I heard them, I wanted to leap out of my shoes.

The first time I introduced Mr. Brown I said, "It's Star Time, The Hardest Working Man in Show Business!.."

I went through the introduction and Bam! I just wanted to exit left.

Brown came up to me afterward and said, "No, it was your first time. You'll be just fine."

I went and got one of those reel-to-reel recorders. I wanted to record the introduction until I got it right. I would listen to myself over and over again. I would keep messing with it.

Someone said to me, "You have to practice until you get things straight."

It worked out fine.

We traveled a lot on the bus. We worked every night.
It gave me a chance to work on my job. Each time you do it
you add more "grip" to yourself. When you hear yourself,
you can make adjustments and start to project your voice
better. All of these things started coming together: the
words, the lyrics, everything. That is your time on stage.
That is something that I had always wanted to do anyway.
I have always wanted to be center stage, ya know? When I
left Birmingham, Alabama, performing for a living is what
I wanted to do.

I believe this was all around 1964. We recorded,
Revolution of the Mind about that time.

We were talking to Syd Nathan with King Records.

He said to Brown, "What are you going to cut now
Jimmy?"

Brown told him, "Same thing I've been doing. I ain't
heard it yet."

He turned to Syd Nathan and said, "We are going to do
a live album."

Syd spoke down to Mr. Brown.

"Live album? I ain't never heard anybody do a 'live'
album before. If you are going to do it, you are going to do
it on your own. You take it out of your own money – out of
your own pocket."

Brown's knees started to shake.

I said to myself, "Oh Lord, he has something cookin."
We came back from practicing and he had the whole

theater wired, the stage, the audience, everything. Shoot man, he had to cut that live album.

I began, "Ladies and gentlemen, it's Star Time!"

You must look for the dramatic dynamics. You go right to the audience, you know. You got to get them up. You must get them involved. You must get the band involved. You must get the whole house involved. This has to happen because James Brown is going to come out on stage like a rocket. That is when everything starts to happen.

He had done another album at the Apollo Theater live. It jumped off the charts. The second time, Bamm! It was a hit right away.

James Brown was the haaaaarrrrrrdddddest working man in show business. You had to put those dynamics into every word. 'The Amaaaaaazing Mr. Please, Please, Please...I want to ask you one thing? Are you ready for some suuuper, dyyyynooomite soul? Because right about now it is star time!'

Please, Please, Please was written in the late 1950s. It was done long before I got there. He and Bobby Byrd did that song. The cape routine starts when he would end the show with Please, Please, Please. That was the last thing we would say in his show. He would do that thing - our routine could last almost 30 minutes. He would come back for an encore.

We were doing what was called the Chitlin circuit then. When you are done performing you would exit stage and go outside. You would then go downstairs and enter the dressing room. He was all wet; he had sweated profusely during his performance. I would put a Turkish towel around him as he went outside. I would take it off and then he would go back out to the audience. We did that a few times.

Later, I told him, "You know what? We got a do this in color!"

That is when we started with the capes. We wanted everything in color. The audience would look for us. They didn't know when, but they knew we were going to do the cape. That was my idea, but everybody kicked in with it. That is when it started happening. It happened right there, bang! We started using different colors for the cape. I think we had about 10 or 15 capes. Some we gave to the Rock'n'Roll Hall of Fame. We gave some to Dick Clark. We've given a few to different people for different things.

When I left and went to the Grammy awards. I took a cape with me. I was just going to show it to them. The BET network honored James Brown. Michael Jackson came on stage. Mr. Bobbit came and talked to me. He said that James Brown was going to put the cape on Michael. I was thinking to myself, 'No, no, no.'

I told him, there are three capes you don't touch: Superman, Batman, and Danny Ray. We don't give up no capes! I was going to fight over that cape. He just stood there looking at me standing offstage. I winked at him and said okay. He was holding it all polite.

I grabbed the cape and said to everyone around me, "Watch."

I told that guy with the camera to 'keep an eye on me.'

He asked me what I was going to do. I told him to wait and see.

I was going to seize the moment. It was a one-time thing. If it was ever going to go down, this would be the time. This was the real deal.

I came up with the cape behind Michael and placed it on his shoulders. That made him dance – he couldn't stand still. The house just fell in. That is what they wanted. That is what they are looking for. The point is you have to have an explosion out there on the stage. If it's going to happen, that is where you want it: right on stage. You never let the energy cease. You've got to keep the explosion going.
We traveled everywhere. Shoot, I just got my fifth passport. We have gone from Moscow to Nigeria then to Hong Kong, China. You name it - we've been there. We've traveled all over Africa. People have stopped wars to see him perform. They sure did. I remember when we got off the plane you could see nothing. Cameras were all going on and they were trying to hold the people back. It was something else. They knew James Brown was coming. Everyone was like that. They were looking for him. He was

a world traveler. Spain, Portugal, Israel. We've been everywhere on the map.

The world audience loved it. It was amazing the way they always greeted us. When you landed you knew what time it was. It was Showtime. There were a lot of smiling faces. That is always good to know that you are welcome.

When James Brown started in the 1950s we had Jim Crow laws. That's what I'm trying to tell you. I joined them in the 1960s and it was still going on. There were a lot of places where you would go and you wouldn't be welcome. It was Jim Crow. We played a lot of gigs where there was separation. But the whites would show up anyway. We played at schools, different gigs, the whites would show up anyway. You could see that the whole change was coming about. That is why we used to call it the Chitlin circuit. We were told, 'don't do this, don't do that.' There's a lot of stuff like that going on. I knew that it was going to wear off.

We played with Peter, Paul, and Mary in Charlotte, North Carolina. We had two shows with them. We worked a lot of shows with white people. It didn't make no difference. The kids would come in and see that "new cool." There was a whole revolution thing going on. It was a whole new thing. We would go to London and experience the same thing. The whole world, man. The whole world was thinking different. When we came back home we would work the show. The change happened all around us. We lived for change. We made the change.

If there was ever competition on stage, Mr. Brown would say, "Mr. Ray, we got to cut them."

He didn't care who it was. They had to go away. He had to be the best. We had to do our part. If they got hurt, I'm sorry. But, 'I got to do what I got to do.' And, of course, 'you've got to do what you've got to do.'

We had to come out working; if you don't sweat, you're not working. You are going to sweat when you went to work with James Brown. Oh yeah - lots of sweat.

If something went wrong on stage, he would cut it off right there in the show. He would turn around and fine you. He would fine you man.

He said, "I would rather fine you than fire you."

That is why we had two of everything. If one member missed something, they might be gone. If someone was out of tune, he would stop everything and say, "I've got a tune this man up. He's out of tune. This man is out of key."

The whole idea was, "Keep your eye on me!"

If he would catch you looking off - "Bam, cut that." Everybody would stop and you would be messing up. The band would look at you and know you were not watching. There would go the fine.

Sometimes he would say, after everyone was done getting dressed, "I'm not fining you. You made a mistake, you need to watch tonight."

He would then have the band member stand in the
wing and watch and see what's happening. That is why he
had two of everything. He would allow the other member
to play and make you stand there and watch the show.
"Now, you know how it goes" Brown would say.

He didn't have two of me. Some guy tried. I made sure
that I got it right. I wanted to sustain the explosion. I was
never going let another man lead.

People could never anticipate what Mr. Brown was
going to do next. Some of the guys would say, "What are
we going to play? What are we going to do next?"

I would tell them, "You don't know until we get
there."

Brown would say, "I will tell you when we get there
son. Keep your eyes open and watch me."

It was all live. We never did any backup tracks. That
stuff came later - but we never did it. In our band, you had
to know what you were going to do. You didn't need to
worry about being perfect because you already were. At
rehearsal in the afternoon everything was worked out.

He would bring sections of the band together before
the show. He was going to be involved "on the One." He
would put the rhythm section in one place, the horns in
another place, the backup singers in another place and then
he would give each one of them their different parts. It
might have looked stupid to someone who didn't know

what was going on. But he knew how to bring it all together.

Nobody was closer to James Brown than me. We were real tight. He would come over to the house and we would talk about a lot of things. I knew his mother and his father. He knew my father and mother, same thing. We would talk about the shows and anything else on his mind. He would talk about things that were coming up. We would talk, laugh, and joke. We always kept that relationship going on. When you work with somebody close like that, you know how to follow their lead.

When he got that new jet plane, Lord have mercy! Sometimes I would keep the hotel keys in my pocket. He took us on a flight from Augusta, Georgia, to Baltimore, and then over to Nashville. We traveled a lot working on those three radio stations. Sometimes we would travel in advance to where we were playing.

That made for a lot of stories. He would come by the house and tell me stories. We got to know a lot of people. On our days off, we would travel to a lot of different places. He would look up at me and say, "Where you at? I know you are around here somewhere."
We were always thinking about the next thing. He would come up with different songs. He would write different tunes down. When he liked something he wrote it down. He couldn't wait to get to the job. That is where it started, on the plane. And he would take it straight to the job. If it was

195

good enough he would say, "We've got to go cut that record tonight."

Right after the show that night we would go to the studio. We would lay the track down. He didn't want to forget about it. He wanted to keep it together.

He was always creating and doing new things all the time. He was always moving. James Brown did not know how to stop. That would not have worked. It was about creating all the time.

He didn't listen to much music of others. He did like Louis Armstrong. He liked a lot of the Blues. But, he mostly liked to create his own thing. It was always about his own thing.

Back in the 1950s and 1960s, a lot of bands would get together and perform: The Drifters, The Flamingos - all of those different groups. There was always something going on at the Apollo Theater. There were performances all day long. Sometimes they would do comedy acts. Even James Brown changed that. They might want to do three or four shows in the day and he would say, "It's not going to be like that."

Instead of doing three or four shows, he said he was only going to do one show. He changed the Apollo Theater! They said no (when he told them he was just going to do one show) so he turned around and walked out of the theater with his crowd.

They stopped him and said, "No. We can work something out."

He wanted to have control of the show in everything. He was the first one to have his own band. Back in the day they wanted you to use their band. You couldn't have your own band. It would take him a week to break their band in - that wasn't for him. He had to have his own band.

He said to the Apollo, "I'll tell you what, we are going to rent the theater. You can have it a week and I can have it a week."

It got to be so the lines would go three or four times around the block. He was always coming up with a new idea about something. The same thing happened with the old Madison Square Garden. I asked him how we were going to work the Garden.

He said, "We're going to do a show on the Fourth of July. That's good. I will take the Fourth of July."

He forgot that people were coming home on the Fourth of July. They didn't want to go somewhere. We still sold it out. It was the old Garden - the one on 50th St. We played there two or three times. We started playing arenas and all. That opened up a whole new world for us. People didn't think he had the guts to do that. They thought he could only work the clubs. He went to work every night. Shoot. When we worked the arenas we had to work at it a different way. That is a whole different engine. The arenas are a different game.

James Brown changed the whole game. He did things differently to move records. He did TV shows like Soul Train. He was a black man on a white man's show with Dick Clark. He changed the whole music game around.

We started working the Beaches. We went everywhere.

Some people would say to us, "Is that where you are going to work?"

He would say, "Yeah."

But then we found out we could only get one or two jobs that way.

He said to me, "That ain't going to work. Let's get the map out. Let's check every town."

We went down the map, A town, B town, C town. He always had to work. He needed to get those jobs promoted.

He used to make records out of the old acetate. They were the 45s. Shoot, we used to cut a whole lot of them up. He would put them in the radio stations. He got the jocks playing his music. He was creating demand. He created demand, and the next thing you know, people were bringing him to town to play a show. He knew if he got the records in the hands of the jocks, people would demand a show. He was always coming up with something new to make sure people were keeping interested. We would come in and work those shows. Shoot.

We worked the Beaches the same way. We started in Virginia, Beach and worked our way all the way down to Florida. Someone would say, "We got a big old empty lot over there. We can run a power line from the highway. We can put a stage over there. We can advertise for the weekend."

Shoot, we had cars lined up for miles to come and see us. That was before integration was going on. We had cars lining up down the whole highway; especially if they advertised it. That was a time if they could eat at Barbecue Chucks or get some soul food. You know they were going to bring food to the show.

There would be a line of people all over the place. We charge $.99 for kids. Brown knew that if a man had a bunch of kids, he couldn't afford a good time. If we charged $.99, a man could bring his family. Brown liked that. We had a lot of fun doing that.

It was fun working all of those places. We liked working the theaters. We knew people would show up. We worked a lot of shows. It was back in a time of Otis Redding and Little Richard. They came out of Macon, Georgia. It was 221 5th St., Macon, GA. That is where we used to work the club. That is where Little Richard saw James and the Flames. Once James Brown made it, then came Otis Redding following in his footsteps. James Brown is the one that got it that started. That was a lot of fun in Macon, Georgia.

Mr. Brown has given me a lot of things over the years. My favorite thing may have been one of the capes. I have put most of those things away. I haven't put that cape away.

We used that in a film: One More Time for the Last Time. There are little things that he gave me that you want to keep.

At his funeral, I put a cape over his coffin. Everybody broke down and cried.

If Mr. Brown was ever upset with his girlfriends or his wife, he would come to my house and we would sit and talk. He would come by the old house. We all had our ups and downs. I kept him out of jail a couple times. I would keep him calmed down. We used to get in trouble together when we were young.

James Brown made the Black and Brown's food stamps. He spent $1 million to help people. You could trade in the book of stamps for three bucks or you could take them and get food and groceries.

Sometimes Mr. Brown had domestic problems. He would come over to the house and I would say, "Come on in, but I don't want to get involved."

I told him that I loved 'all y'all.' I would tell him, "When you get back together, you will compare stories and say this or that. I don't want to take sides."

She would show up and I would say, "I got to keep you in the house."

They would get back together and we would laugh about it. But I had to keep him calmed down. He would drive over here and eventually everybody would calm down. I think that's why he came here so often, because he knew that I was going to referee it right. It was just a misunderstanding. I didn't want to get into his business.

When you're out there together on the road, things just happen. Mostly good things. Something is going to come about. Sometimes he would call me up and say, "You got a try this." I told him that I didn't want to try none of that. Some things you just don't do. We laughed about it.

We laughed about a lot of stuff. I was in Seattle once with Mr. Brown when he has me come down to his room. He said to 'take these two elephants (women)' out of his room. We laughed about that.

When you're on the road, crazy like that happens. It makes you stop and think about things. It was always about tomorrow though. We can't get hung up on yesterday. It won't work. It won't work at all. We would laugh about things that happened on the road and just move on to the next stop.

When you're on the road and moving you don't have time to get mad and stay in one place. It's good to just get up and move on. That is the best thing to do. If you got to move, you don't have to wait around nowhere. You can get up and be gone.

I stayed with him because I liked being on the road. I liked the business. I liked the man. I liked creating things together. It was an adventure. We met people we never thought we would meet. It was always an adventure. We

201

met Sammy Davis Jr. out in California. All of them entertainers were the same way too.

People looked at me and said I look just like Sammy Davis Jr. I got to know him real well. We got to go to the Copacabana in New York together. We played there. They wanted us to stay two weeks. We had a chance to go back to the Apollo Theater, and we had to go back. Bootsy Collins came and played with us there with the band. We had a lot of fun.

Bootsy Collins played real good; him and his other brother, Catfish. Bootsy was about 15 or 16 years old when he first started with James Brown. That is when they joined the band. That is when he put both bands together.

I got the got a chance to meet Sherman Helmsley. I met Dan Aykroyd and really liked him. We met Siegfried and Roy in Las Vegas. I didn't want to be close to that tiger. I told them I would stay back. No cat is going to come near me.

I remember performing with the Jewels. Their performance ran long. Mr. Brown was sensitive about those kinds of things. He kicked them off stage.

The Flames were not happy with James Brown when he changed the name. But we had to do what we had to do. The band started out as the Famous Flames.

Rocky IV - that is where we performed Living in America. We did that with a black fighter, Carl Weathers.

Stallone asked for us to come and do the film, that was the first time I met Rocky. I had never met Rocky before. That is where I met Phyllis Diller as well.

I was sitting offstage and the producers came to me and said, "You got to get down in the picture. You are too dressed up not to be doing something."

I went down and started talking to Rocky. He told me to do that cape routine. I told him that I sure will. I told him that I appreciated him. He said don't worry about a thing. He signed a picture for me. I told him I sure appreciated it. He told me not to worry about it man.

We spent a whole week there with him. We spent a whole week with Robin Williams as well. I met him at an international soccer thing. The event was in Las Vegas.

I remember being in the Super Bowl in New Orleans. We were the halftime act. I introduced Mr. Brown the same way I had for years. Got to do it right. You've got to give the people what they're looking for. Don't change things up. Give them what they want. If you change, they won't recognize you. Stay the same.

Brown didn't treat me any differently than the other band members. He would be tough on me if I messed up. I had to keep it straight. I always like to stay on top of things. I had to be creative. I was always saying, "Let's get busy."

He always had more background singers than he really needed. He would say, "Everybody needs a job."

The last time I played with Brown was in Indonesia. When promoters would book James Brown they had to have me. I was a big part of the show. They got to know me. They knew me for my voice. They wanted me to come with my voice. They wouldn't allow any substitutes to get on that stage. It had to be me.

Brown read the Bible all the time. He would be in the book. We would always say a prayer before we went on stage. We always prayed. Definitely. We were thankful to be there. We would pray and give thanks. We would be grateful to be there safely. Shoot. He would always give thanks. We all prayed together. Every one of us. We had no problem about that - we had no problem about a prayer.

I miss him. Oh yeah I miss him. I definitely do. No doubt about it. Think about him every day. No doubt about it. Every day was a new adventure with James Brown. It sure was. I would like to think that he's looking out for me, I sure would. Every day we would wake up and think of something new. We would think about going someplace new. Think about doing something new.

***

My memories of the band

My father changed the whole game when it comes to music. He wrote the whole book. Wilt Chamberlain changed the game of basketball and my father change the game of music. He was a musical icon – a musical savant.

When you talk about Funk, new grooves, R&B - all of those different words came from my father, James Brown. These ideas and musical forms came from Augusta, Georgia. There was a church called the "Right On" Augusta Church. When he came out with that song, "Papa's Got a Brand-new Bag", that changed the whole R&B, top 40, Funk, everything. James Brown did that. James Brown brought the funk to the people. He brought it before Sly Stone. It was James Brown who helped people become aware of their soul.

James Brown put a focus on un-natural rhythms. His focus was the one and the three. You could be deaf and you would still tap your feet to James Brown.

Jet Magazine does soul charts and hit single charts. Those are my father's - they belong to my father. Motown didn't seek to destroy my father; they were just competitive with him. It was a friendly rivalry. When you have one man selling more records than your entire record label, of course Motown wanted to take down my father. He had a small record label and was making more money than all of Motown. They had writers, arrangers, and promoters - they were a great label.

My dad always believed in the underdog, the little guy, the small business owner. He did not like the largest record labels. He sacrificed millions of dollars to sign with smaller labels. He wanted autonomy, creative license, and a significant voice on all major decisions. He believed that was the right thing to do. He was not going to betray his convictions for any amount of money.

He produced "Live at the Apollo" by himself. Sid Nathan did not want to give him the money to do that album. He told my father he would not give him the money up front. Microphones were put all over and under the stage. You could even hear somebody fart. It was one of the biggest sellers of all time.

Back in 1968 or 1969 my father, Mr. Dynamite, and my grandfather, came to New Brunswick, New Jersey to visit me and my mother. They stirred up the whole damn place. There were so many people surrounding the house that we couldn't even walk in. James Brown attracted a crowd wherever he went. He bought me a drum set and a guitar. That is how I ended up playing guitar.

My grandfather would tell everybody, including my father, "One day, James, that boy is going to be in your band."

It didn't happen until I was 40 years old - but it happened. I was going to go in as a drummer. It ended up that I would play the guitar. I haven't put the guitar down since.

As you can imagine, growing up I always held a grudge against my father. I didn't have him around. I missed him and I really didn't know him. There is something special about a boy and his father and I missed that growing up. When I got older, I started letting it go. I understood who this man was. I started looking at all the things that I didn't do right. It became difficult for me to judge that man. I had a father, and then I had 'James Brown', my boss. He was harder on me than anybody in the band.

I was there when he did Revolution of the Mind. I was a valet every summer. I took care of the clothes and the shoes. It was like a Chinese laundry. It was my summer job. I was a nervous wreck doing that job, but I had the chance to work for the man, James Brown! He never demanded from anyone else things that he was not willing to demand from himself. He tried to help the band understand that they were representing him.

When James Brown wanted to make a point, show his power, he would open up the auditions; particularly for new drummers. He would always take me with him. I thought I was always good enough to get one of these drum spots. Cool. That's what I'd do.

He would have me play a song and then he would have the person auditioning play the song. All along he was just using me. He was making a point to the regular drummer. He was trying to let them know they were dispensable. He could have a new drummer tomorrow. I would play the song and then the other guy would play the song. I knew the songs. The other guy would be sweating. He was trying to figure it out. I knew the song like I knew the back of my hand.

He would say to them, "If I'm going to hire anybody, I'm going to hire my son. But…I'm going to keep my other drummer."

It was a nice thing he said about me. But I was just being used. He would do this all the time. When he told me I was good to be his third guitar player, I couldn't sleep for two nights. I didn't know if he was telling me the truth. I knew I was going to catch hell for being in the band. I had to be good. I wanted to be great.

The hard part for me was I had been playing drums for 30 years. I learned how to play the guitar in an interesting way. We started talking about an old acoustic guitar he had in a box. He told me to go get it. He said it was in the attic. I went and climbed up into the attic and got the acoustic. He sat at the piano and I started playing the guitar. We were jamming together.

He said to me, "Man! I have never heard any rhythm like that. You're going to be my third guitar player."

I had been waiting for years, even decades to get the drum spot and now he was going to have me play the guitar? Crazy man.

I played in the band with my father for about eight years. I played lead guitar. I was the only child to grace the stage with him.

He loved me because I could harmonize whatever note he sang. I knew his music. I have that talent. Whatever he wanted me to do, I would do it. It was much harder to play the guitar because I was a drummer. I could also play the keyboard.

He asked me one day, "Who taught you how to use your left hand?"

It was my sister Venetia. She taught me. Unfortunately, she got into drugs. It's too bad. If we could have had the three of us in the studio it would've been a slam dunk. She was spectacular.

I used to put up with his harshness. That all changed. We were on a trip to New York, and he was tripping. He was high. He looked around for me and I was gone. I have the same temper as James Brown. There was a few times where I wanted to take the guitar and bash it over my father's head. He was mean to me man - mean.

I had just signed an endorsement deal with one of the best guitar companies in the world. I told Charles Bobbit about the endorsement. My dad thought the same company would now come to him for a deal. It wasn't that way. This was about me. He thought I was getting too big for my britches. He had to be in control. I couldn't even use my father's guitar. It was a $5000 guitar. I had to use other cheaper guitars.

I had a different guitar it was cheaper. It was black, just like his. It was worth $200. I knew how to work him. I called the company and had them send me the very best guitar they had but painted black - just like his. I knew how to get the man - and I did.

This is how I would get back to my father when he was terrible to me on the stage: The very next night I would do the song bigger and better than anything he asked for. He couldn't say anything to that. A lot of the parts I played in the band, I made up. He would tell everybody they were his. Not so. They were mine. It was in my blood. But I had to let my ego go. Ego will get you broke.

What changed my life was that I actually had to go to prison. I had to put up with all of their shit. I had to do what I was told by the C.O. I knew this is where I was going to have to grow up. I knew that if I could put up with the shit in prison, I could put up with my father, James Brown. I learned not to get even with people in prison. Sometimes you just let it be.

The whole thing about being a bandleader was just maintaining control. Musicians are hard to deal with. When they played as hard as they could play, they felt like their name should be on the marquee. He would put them back in their place. It was his name on the marquee. It's the James Brown band. His name is in lights - not yours. This was not about you. That was the business. It was not personal. It was straight up business.

On occasion, there were divisions in the band; sometimes along the lines of race. It was difficult for some. They failed to remember that it was the James Brown band. My father was the headline act. The band, if they were included, would be a subtitle.

Most of the time life was good, and they would get together as various groups of friends and smoke a little weed. I miss playing with the band. We were the best band on the planet.

My father often talked about his trip to Vietnam. When my dad went to Vietnam to entertain the troops, he paid for it himself. He didn't do a USO tour. He was upset because they wouldn't take his full band. They cut his band in half. All he wanted to do was serve his country. Ali wanted to run from Vietnam – my father wanted to run toward Vietnam. He had no fear. He wanted soldiers of color to be treated equally. He wanted all of the troops to have music that moved their body and soul. Nobody was more patriotic than James Brown. He was getting shot at. He was getting shot at while in the plane. I don't remember Bob Hope entertaining the troops and getting shot at.

He would make a joke of it. He was upset they couldn't have guns. He knew how to use a rifle. He asked whoever was in charge, "Please, at least give me a stick or something!" He was always ready for a fight.
I remember once when I had swollen glands. I did not want to perform. However, when you get on stage and in the groove, it's like a drug. Performing helps you to feel better. You don't feel any pain. As soon as I got off stage, and covered up in a blanket, it hit me like a ton of bricks. I was a young kid when it happened. My father was an old man

and never complained. He never missed a show. I never understood that about my father.

As my father got older I knew he was in a lot of pain. He had arthritis. If you look in his medicine cabinet it looked like the medicine cabinet of an athlete. He had creams, gels, everything to relieve pain. That is why he took drugs; to relieve the pain. He was performing like a 20-year-old athlete on stage for more than 50 years. He didn't want to take pills. His body hurt so much. He would never complain about the pain.

I remember one time when he was in South America. They had to put a catheter in his body so that he could go to the bathroom. The promoters told him to take a couple of days off. We made arrangements to come back into the show later. My father said 'no!' He went on the stage the next night and did the show.

He tried to do the splits one night when we were in London. I think at the Tower of London Festival in July of 2006. He had to see if he could do it. He was in his 70s if I remember correctly. He got hurt. They had to help him get up. It was at the end of the show after Sex Machine. That is who he was. He was the same performer in later years that people loved during the 60s and 70s. He believed the audience deserved his very best. It was sincere; it was from his heart.

***

Pavarotti & Friends - **Man's, Man's, Man's, World**

James Brown revered Pavarotti. Sharing a stage would never have been considered by Brown as a younger man. However, the Godfather of Soul enthusiastically embraced the opportunity to sing with arguably the greatest tenor in history. Their soulful and somewhat sad rendition of Man's, Man's, Man's World is one of the greatest duets of all time. Pavarotti had experienced personal loss that year. His eyes sorrowfully gazed into an unknown universe. The audience longed for understanding. His part, sung in Italian, provide a clear juxtaposition for the greatness of James Brown as both a performer and a vocalist. As a man of contradiction, this may have been Brown's very best.

George "Spike" Nealy II

I played with James Brown and Pavarotti in 2002. I was definitely there. It was in Medina, Italy. We got there and checked into the hotel. We had a little time to relax. There was so much going on with the different artists on the show. Everybody was slotted for different rehearsal times.

We went over to the venue. It was a huge, huge, production. We had a 75 piece orchestra playing with us. Before performing Man's World, we ran through a quick medley of James Brown tunes - about a fifteen to twenty minute show. We didn't have to practice for it, that's what we do every night.

After rehearsal, he said, "Gentlemen, we'll see you back here. After I finish this I am gonna do Man's World."

They needed to wipe the stage off after we exited. Then, the 75 piece orchestra and James Brown came on to do Man's World.

At that moment, immediately after we had just finished rehearsing our part, they were wiping the stage off and were taking the amps and everything off. The band had exited and went down the side of the stage. Someone came to move my percussion. I said to myself, 'Hey, no way I'm going - no way am I leaving this stage now. No way!'

Playing with this 75 piece orchestra - Pavarotti, the King of what he does and James Brown, the King of what he does - no way am I going to leave this stage.

I told the crew, "Hey man, don't touch my equipment."

I look to the side and I see some of the guys in the band.

They said, "Hey man, come on. You gotta get off stage."

No way! I wasn't leaving the stage.

So, by that time, they hurried and went on back to the dressing room. I stood there. I made sure I had my cymbal and everything, cause I knew he was gonna play Man's World. So I had my cymbal and my Cuíca - everything was ready for Man's World.

In the meantime, Pavarotti walks out. James Brown walks out. He didn't see me at first. He walked out and all of a sudden he starts singing Man's World. After Man's World, I KNOW Mr. Brown looked over there and saw me. I had the look on my face letting him know, "Let's go!"

We got to go – let's do it! Let's do it now!

Brown started singing and then Pavarotti did his part. I told myself, 'If I'm outta here, I might as well go out with a bang.' I would never get this moment again to do what I did with two geniuses on stage at the same time.

After we got through, sang the last song, hit the last note, big swell at the end, wait for the holler and scream, right there and then I did a big cymbal swell. I heard the song cut off and everybody on the technical crew stood up clapping! That was just rehearsal!

Mr. Brown turned and left the stage. Pavarotti turned and left the stage.

The technical crew said, "Gentlemen, we are going to strike the stage."

I went down into the dressing room. As I was sitting there, the band was just waiting for the hammer to drop. They knew it was trouble. At that moment came a knock on the dressing room door.

"Mr. Brown wants to see Mr. Nealy."

Ohhhh boy, here we go. I took a good deep breath of air and walked down the hallway. I knocked on his door.

"Who is it?"

I said, "It's me Mr. Brown, it is Nealy."

I heard him reply, "Come in son."

I went in. He was under the hair dryer.

I said, "Mr. Brown (before he starts talking I start talking), I know why you called me in here. Mr. Brown, I'm just going to apologize. Right away sir. There was just no way for me to leave the stage with a song that powerful. I definitely wanted to be there to give you the support that I knew I could bring to the song and give it to you."

He said, "Son, what are you talkin' about?"

I'm standing there with my mouth open because of what he said.

I told him, "I figured you had called me here for being on stage."

He said, "Son, I didn't call you here for that, I think it was great, I'll see you on stage tonight! Mr. Nealy, when the band leaves the stage, make sure the crew leaves your stuff on stage and you be there for when I perform Man's World."

When I got back to the dressing room, everybody was wondering, "What did he say? What axe did he use to chop your neck off?"

I really didn't tell the band that it was okay. At the performance that particular night, it actually went down with me playing percussion. After our set, the band exited to go to the dressing rooms. The technical crew did the sweep of the stage. They had four chairs for the girls singing background. They were sitting right by the orchestra. When the song started, it was the girls, James

Brown, myself, Pavarotti, and a 75 piece orchestra. That tape will go down in history.

That's exactly what happened, and now both gentlemen are dead. I told people that they needed to make a DVD. It was the only performance of Man's World that was sung in Italian and English at the same time. Pavarotti sung his part in Italian and Mr. Brown sung his part in English. Now, both men are dead. That song was an instant classic.

I remember after the show, the young guy who wrote the orchestration on Man's World. He was so excited, writing it for Mr. Brown. He wanted to go to the dressing room and meet Mr. Brown and give him the whole score. We got him to the dressing room and he gave Mr. Brown the score.

In my 15 years of going through three passports, crossing every ocean that can be crossed, performing on every continent on earth, clocking more than 300 shoes each year for 15 straight amazing, educational, incredible, but mostly unbelievable years with the hardest working man in show business I feel nothing but gratitude. As a percussionist, Mr. James Brown gave me a canvas to color and paint - that was his music. People gave him a canvas to color and that canvas was the world.

(Spikeology) The study of making the heart smile, through the art of entertainment.

***

From Georgia to Georgia

Among the pantheon of performers – James Brown had no equal among entertainment deities until he personally passed the baton to his pupil Michael Jackson.

In 1964 Mick Jagger and the Rolling Stones had top billing on the T.A.M.I show. Brown was not just disappointed, he was angry. Those unfamiliar with James Brown had no idea how competitive he was. Outwardly, Brown was relaxed, cool, and animated. Inwardly, he was angry, aggressive, and ready to attack. That night, Mick was good; James was sensational. Yet again, he felt he had something to prove.

Self-doubt can be devastating - yet with Brown it was ever-present. Induction into the initial class of the Rock'n'Roll Hall of Fame should have removed all uncertainty. Truly brilliant performers are wired differently; he never fully understood that he was the One.

A rare opportunity emerged to make a splash in the former Soviet Republic of Georgia. Brown seized the day. Those in attendance witnessed a spectacular finish - one that will be told for generations to come. James always sent the audience home on his terms. He would pass away within months.

***

Hollie Farris

I was right in the middle of the famous Georgia experience. This was not Augusta, Georgia - this was Soviet Georgia. I remember we were doing a sound check. There was a huge Olympic size swimming pool in front of us. They built this stage on one end of the Olympic pool high above the water. On the other side of the Olympic pool they built bleachers, the stands.

It almost appeared as though we were performing at a swimming race. Here we were on one side of the pool, and the audience was entirely on the other side. During the sound check James kept walking up to the edge of the stage - to the edge of the pool - he would look down at the water. I thought to myself, this man can't possibly think he's going to jump into the pool. He was definitely afraid of water. He almost drowned when he was a child. He had a pool at his house that he never swam in. He was afraid of water. Yet, he kept walking up to the edge of the stage and looking down. It was at least a 12-foot drop, a long way down.

He walked up to me and said, "Mr. Farris, if I jump into that pool, will you come in and get me? I need you to help me get out."

I told him that I would. I said I would be right behind him.

I knew full well he was not going to jump. He was afraid of water. Sure enough, on the last song, Sex Machine, he hauls off and jumps into the middle the pool. He started to swim over to the audience. He made it just a few strokes and then he started to sink. By this time, I had managed to get my shoes and coat off and I dove in after him. I dragged him back to the side of the pool and then - I started to sink! By this time, enough of the people who jumped into the pool started to help him up. Yes, I got to him first. I could not believe it. His cowboy boots filled up with water and he sank like a rock…he took a couple of strokes and then he was underwater.

When I grabbed him he had that look of, "Thank God! Somebody has just saved my life!" He had a look of terror in his eyes. He just wanted out of the water. He never said anything about me saving his life. He didn't have to.

Everybody that jumped into the pool got a bonus that night. It was $150 or $200.

***

George "Spike" Nealy II

I was in Soviet Georgia when he jumped into the pool. Yes, I was there. As a matter of fact, it was Robert Thompson on drums, myself, and Fred - we were about the only three or four people that did not jump into the water. I'm up on a riser far behind the pool. I was about three feet above Mousey, the drummer.

First of all, James Brown asked when he got to town, "What did the last band do that was amazing? What did the last artist do when he ended the show?"

220

The person responded, "Oh, Mr. Brown, they got a standing ovation, they just clapped and clapped, they did about two encores."

He simply said, "Okay."

But he had that look on his face. I knew when they told him that, it was a challenge. We were going to go out with a bang. I didn't know what kind of bang - I had no idea what he had in mind.

James Brown is afraid of water. He doesn't even play with water. He didn't travel in a boat. There was none of that. I even told the stage manager to make sure that they put an extra piece of reflective tape at least three feet before the end of the stage, and then put another inches before the end, just so he could see it. If he gets past the end of the tape he would know that he was headed toward the water.

They put the tape at the end as we requested. We did a great show. Everybody was clapping hard and screaming. Next thing I know, I open my eyes and we're performing Sex Machine. He didn't back up, he went all the way toward the edge of the stage. I thought to myself, 'Okay, I know what he is going to do.' He is getting ready to run to the front, twist his jacket as if he is getting ready to throw it. I have seen this act before. He will run toward the end of the stage and throw his jacket back.
As the audience sees him running they think they know what he is going to do. I have a better idea. But, I don't see him take the jacket off. He started running and I'm

wondering how he is going to take his jacket off while running?

He was getting closer and closer to that microphone. I knew he would stop when he saw the white line. Man! When I saw him go past that white line my eyes got big as a quarter. I looked at Mousey and Mousey looked back at me. We were still playing Sex Machine. I said to myself, 'Even if he tried to stop right now, he's not going to be able to stop.' The next thing I know, he is just like one of those cartoons. Do you remember when a character ran out in the air? Straight down…shoop.

Man, I saw him go straight down. I'm not talking about a thirteen or fourteen foot drop. I am talking about 20 feet. We were at the top of the Olympic diving board. We were way up there. The next thing I know, the dancers that were on both sides of the stage went in. By the time he hit the water the dancers were right there behind him. Then the horn players hit the water and everybody else in the band followed by diving into the water. Nobody took off their uniforms. They had on shoes, socks, tuxedoes, everything! That was an amazing night, I guess he was definitely number one, leaving you with a bang! That's number one in everybody's mind!

***

<u>Robert "Mousey" Thompson</u>

Nealy and I were too far back. Our kits were elevated on the risers. I can't believe Brown did that with boots on.

He turned around to me and said, "I'm jumping in." I kept playing. You know James, the next thing I know he runs and jumps in this pool with his boots on and everybody is diving in. Dancers followed and then the horns. I don't know who else jumped. I think the other drummer may have jumped in. The only thing I didn't get was that bonus! He gave everybody I think a 200 dollar bonus.

Hollie Farris, Music Director.

Lifelong friend, Rev. Al Sharpton.

Daryl Brown and his dad, The Godfather of Soul.

Promotional photo of the tour that never was.

William Murrell and the van that he used to transport James Brown's body to the Apollo Theatre in Harlem, New York from Augusta, Georgia.

George "Spike" Nealy II and James Brown.

Danny Ray the Cape Man.

Rest in Peace, The Final Act, we all miss him.

Keith Graham, the Bodyguard.

James Brown and the stunning Adrienne Brown.

The one and only…
George "Spike" Nealy II.

Donald Danner.

The Ford truck that was riddled with dozens of bullet holes by the South Carolina Police Department.

James Brown was born in and grew-up in extreme poverty.

James Brown, The Godfather of Soul.

Brown-Chabries/My Father the Godfather

Mr. Dynamite.

Daryl Brown, what are you thinking about?

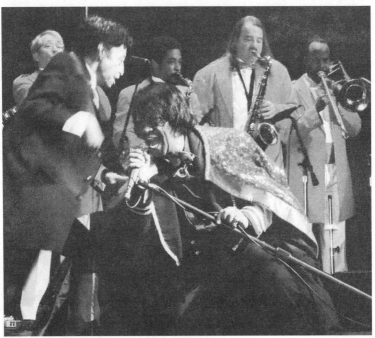

Danny Ray performing his magic.

Brown-Chabries/My Father the Godfather

There will never be another James Brown!

236

The Sex Machine.

Section III
Civil Rights

My father loved Danny Ray. They were hand and glove. Danny Ray has said many times, "When James Brown started in the 1950s we had Jim Crow laws. That's what I'm trying to tell you. I joined them in the 1960s and it was still going on. There were a lot of places where you would go and you wouldn't be welcome. It was Jim Crow.

We played a lot of gigs where there was separation. But the whites would show up anyway. You could see that the whole change was coming about. That is why we used to call it the Chitlin circuit. We were told, don't do this, don't do that. There's a lot of stuff like that going on. I knew that it was going to wear off." It would take James Brown to make the hatred "wear off."

During an episode of the Mike Douglas show in 1969, a polished guest, David Susskind, condescendingly asked my father, "So many people have offered their advice on how the Negro can improve his position in America life. What is your opinion?"

Brown momentarily stumbled through an oft-repeated answer about education, but he quickly regained his balance. His response is still true today. "The first thing is, a man has to be, 'a man.' When you said 'Negro,' this is a term that has been used so many times but I don't particularly care for that term. I would rather be a black

238

man because that is my identity. That is the way we can improve ourselves by having a stronger identity and respect for ourselves as 'a man.' Believing in yourself and wanting to live by the sweat of your own eyebrow. Living with your convictions; not running away from yourself."

I was proud as I watched my daddy on TV, even though I had no idea what he was talking about. He was always "a man" to me.

The answer my father gave that day was simple, honest and profound. I remember that Douglas wanted to move quickly away from this uncomfortable moment with Susskind.

Mike gazed into the air and asked, "Jim, sometimes do you get caught up in the middle of what to say to blacks who want you to be blacker and to whites who want you to be whiter?"

Mr. Brown retorted, "Well, you see it's not a difficult bias for me because I am 'a man' first. I'm a black man because I'm black. But I am 'a man' first so you don't bother me."

First, nobody who really knew my father called him Jim. This was a clear indication you had no idea what you were talking about. Dad didn't play that way. Second, understanding the "South" and how it impacted my father is paramount to understanding James Brown.

Let me paint a picture.

If a man of dignity, character, and education walked into a restaurant and asked for a simple sandwich and glass of lemonade, the owner would carefully study his features, squint to see his pores and consider his kinky hair, eyes, nose, and lips. After staring and measuring for what must have felt like an eternity, the owner could angrily yell, "You better get your black ass out of here boy." This was standard in the South.

Black people were greeted daily by "Whites only" signs and others that read: "No Dogs, Niggers, or Mexicans." Bathrooms were limited to white only customers. Black men would need to relieve themselves behind the service station. Apparently the constitution of a Black man's shit was different than a White's. It may have clogged the sewer system more quickly; that is my best guess.

Jim Crow laws were put in place by Southern and Border States. Think Georgia and South Carolina. These distasteful remnants of segregation emerged just after the Emancipation Proclamation was drafted by Lincoln. "The War of Northern Aggression" as some refer to The Civil War had not decided the question of One Nation, under God, indivisible...Liberty and justice was only for those with white skin.

"Jim Crow" simply meant "Negro", which came from a character in a minstrel song. The character was a buffoon. Crow was often depicted by a white actor covered in makeup or "black face." He was a character you hated to love and therefore you loved to hate.

The United States Supreme Court validated the hatred of Jim Crow in the landmark ruling of Plessy v. Ferguson in 1896. Separate facilities for whites and blacks were considered lawful under the Constitution. Separate was equal. Railways and streetcars, public waiting rooms, restaurants, boardinghouses, theaters, public parks and even churches were segregated; separate schools, hospitals, and other public institutions, generally of inferior quality, were designated only for people of color.

In some sense, the laws of Jim Crow were a reminder that the blood shed during the Civil War was spilled in vain. The "last full measure of devotion" spoken by Lincoln at Gettysburg, only illustrated that the "cause" was an "unfinished work." The fight would continue for another hundred years before my father assumed his place as an advocate of freedom and equality for all. The "Separate but Equal" principle was an absurd legal doctrine that continued the consequences of slavery in the South. "Separate but equal" or segregated schools created a sub-class of citizens that were generally capable of little more than menial labor. Profit was gained at the expense of those who were on the wrong side of "equal." Few escaped the clutches of ignorance.

My father completed no more than the 7th grade. He saw his textbooks were the leftovers of privileged students, so

Brown being Brown, stubbornly closed the books and walked out of school. Manhood would come by walking a different path, but he regretted and was embarrassed that he was not formally educated.

The truth is, formal education policies promoting segregation was little more than readin', writin', and 'rithmatic. The Supreme court agreed in 1955 with the Brown v. Board decision. By then, my father was tearing up the Chitlin circuit and creating hit records. Please, Please, Please was recorded in 1956.

As previously stated, when asked by a London reporter what was more important, "The message or the music?"

My father astutely replied, "The message, but it takes the music to get it in you."

The doctrine of the civil rights movement was canonized by men like Malcolm X and Martin Luther King. However, the message did not penetrate minds and souls of both white and black people until it was associated with the best music in the world. That music belonged to my father.

My father's friend, Buddy Dallas, publicly said, "James Brown was the 'Gabriel's Horn' of the Civil Rights movement. Before Dr. King said, 'We shall overcome' there was James Brown saying, Say it loud. I'm black and I'm proud!"

This metaphor of Gabriel's Horn fits nicely. The horn mathematically has an infinite surface area but limited depth. In other words, my dad had mass appeal. He could

242

penetrate minds and bodies in a way that was not shared by Dr. King. He could penetrate their minds and bodies in a way that was not available to King. However, it was the deeper message of Martin Luther King that inspired so many. My father was simply the messenger. "I would rather die on my feet than live on my knees," he sang.

When asked if James Brown had a greater impact on the expansion of civil rights than Martin Luther King, Charles Bobbit said, "That is 200% correct!"

Of course, Bobbit and my father were life-long friends. Bobby Byrd's wife, Vicki Anderson, doesn't share the same affection for my father. In her mind, James Brown was not cut from the same cloth as Martin Luther King.

"He was motivated by other things."

I would agree, James Brown was cut from different cloth - and people liked it.

After King was assassinated in 1968, the voice of the civil rights was left void. In February of 1969, Look Magazine rhetorically asked on the front cover: "James Brown - Is he the most important black man in America?"

Thomas Berry authored The Importance of Being Mr. James Brown. Berry quoted Buddy Lowe of station XERB in Los Angeles, "He is our lovable entertainer-and our best teacher."

Later, he astutely observed, "His constituency dwarfs Stokely Carmichael's and the late Dr. Martin Luther King's."

My father responded, "I'm a racist when it comes to freedom. I can't rest until the black man in America is let out of jail, until his dollar's as good as the next man's."

This observation would prove prophetic when he was personally incarcerated 20 years later. Both the arrest and prosecution had unmistakable elements of racism. That story will be told later.

Berry continued writing, "To his people, he is a poet, philosopher, benefactor and possible Messiah." He further quoted my father, "I don't say hire a cat cause he's black - just hire him cause he's right. There is an idea of keeping money in the black community. If we can keep the turnover going then 'we shall overcome' - only - if we all come over."

By 1969 the vast majority of black leaders had been assassinated, murdered, or marginalized. He was one of the few black men in America that had a voice consistently heard by the people.

Shortly after the assassination of Martin Luther King Jr., there were several domestic disturbances in cities around the country. My father gave a speech in Washington D.C.

He said, "I guess you know that I started as a shoeshine boy in Augusta, Georgia. I didn't get the chance to finish the 7th grade. But I made it. I made it because you believed in me. I had honesty, dignity, and sincerity. I wanted to be somebody. This is the reason today why I talk to the kids. I tell them to stay in school and not be a dropout. If I hadn't looked up, and because of the goodwill of certain people, I wouldn't be here. Education is the answer. Know what you are talking about. Be qualified. Be ready. Know what you are doing.

You know, when I was in Augusta, Georgia, I used to shine shoes on the steps of the radio station WRDW. I think we started charging three cents and then went up to five and six cents. We never did get to a dime. Today, I own that radio station. Do you know what that is? That is black power (pointing to his brain). Black power is not in violence, it is in knowing what you are talking about. Being ready.

I am saying this to you because I am your brother. I know where it's at. I have been there. I'm not sharing from my imagination; I'm sharing this from my experience. Let's live for our country. (Dramatic pause). Let's live for ourselves! Please go off the street."

My father talked many times about the role he played in squelching public riots, particularly in Boston after the death of Martin Luther King (that was epic) and the race riots in Augusta, Georgia in 1970. Interestingly, 20 years later when my father was sent to prison, he thought the country would riot just as they had for King. He was wrong.

On the morning after the assassination of Dr. Martin Luther King, Boston anticipated a second night of public riots.

245

Boston had served as a second home to King. President Johnson declared a national state-of-emergency. Many cities erupted in violence. While preparing police for a second night of violence, one more variable came to the attention of Mayor Kevin White. It was a risky play - but it may have been his last card if he wanted a peaceful resolution.

James Brown was scheduled to perform in Boston Garden. White used him brilliantly to keep the peace. On the night of April 5, 1968, James Brown performed in concert and the Mayor was insightful enough to televise the concert to every home.

People were glued to their seats. That is exactly what the Mayor wanted.

During the show this is what my father said to the audience. "Give Mayor Kevin White a round of applause - he is a swinging cat. The man is together."

The Boston Garden had an intense moment toward the end of the concert. Enthusiastic young fans, most of them black, jumped up on stage to shake the hand of an American icon. The police quickly stepped in and threw one of the over-eager boys back into the crowd. The rush began and James ordered the police to step back. For some inexplicable reason, they complied, although it would have been reasonable to assume my father was not safe.

After several minutes of telling people "Wait! Go back to your seats," my father patiently said: "Step down son, now, be a gentleman...I asked the police to step back, because I think I can get some respect from my own people. You're making me look bad...You're not being fair to yourself or your own race. I asked the police to step back, because I figured I could get some respect from my own people. It doesn't make sense. Now, are we together or are we ain't?"

He finished the concert and touched hands (he was a germaphobe by the way) with all those in the front rows of the Boston Garden.

I remember him reflecting on the time he brought peace to our hometown of Augusta, Georgia when I was a young boy.

On Monday, May 11, 1970, Charles Oatman, was a teenager held in the county jail. The charge was murder. Charles' mental capacity was significantly limited, a fact well known in the community. He was tortured and killed while in the custody of the sheriff. Violent treatment of black Americans was a common occurrence while incarcerated. Consider the Attica prison riots in 1971. Twenty-nine inmates were killed along with ten hostages. Hundreds of inmates were injured or wounded in some way.

A riot erupted among citizens marching toward the municipal government offices in Augusta, Georgia. Black citizens brought down and subsequently burned the state flag. They burned or looted buildings in the immediate area. Police responded by killing six African American men and wounding twenty-five others. Segregationist Governor, Lester Maddox, deployed the National Guard. He gave the order to "shoot and kill."

On Wednesday, May 13, Jim Whipkey broadcasted the following from Augusta, Georgia on WSB-TV: "Negro entertainer, James Brown, flew into his home town and appeared on television to tell black people, 'cool it.' Brown toured the troubled area asking for calm. Many people said they listened to him and would not have listened to anyone else."

My father was asked on camera, "What advice would James Brown give to anyone who participated in last night's events?"

Dad said, "Well um, I can't give no definite advice. My advice would be to the administration as well as to those who participated. We got to respect each other and we got to talk about it. We are all human beings. I can't tell you to walk away from something that you believe in. I can't tell them to walk away. But I can say we should all walk to the bargaining table and be men and human beings, and find something with immediate reason where we can understand each other. I think it is so important, right now. I'm sure we can agree. The circumstances are bad but it is not like people are losing lives.

It looks like (with the National Guard deployment) that we are going into combat. We don't need no combat here!

Don't nobody want that here. We are hoping to get the best out of it (this bad situation) but it looks like we are going to get the worst out of it." After talking to us, Brown left town and the blacks did cool it. Maybe Brown did do it. Maybe the armed National Guardsman did it, or perhaps there was nothing left they wanted to burn? The fact remains, six men are dead and 51 businesses have been burned, and the usually bustling city of Augusta has been shut down for a night.

From 1956-2001, Georgia proudly incorporated the "Stars and Bars" into the state flag. This may have been an immediate political reaction to the Supreme Court decision making it unlawful to adopt segregation practices in Brown v. Board. Interestingly, CNN reported on April 4, 2014 that Wilcox County High School held their first integrated prom in decades. Wilcox County High is approximately 150 miles from Augusta.

Segregation was simply a reality - the reality - of the world for my father. It was a reality for the Chitlin circuit along the East Coast and in the South. My father's band was repeatedly stopped by police as they traveled from city to city. On more than one occasion he was told to "dance" to the parade of bullets at his feet. If he would have had the chance to take the man one-on- one, he would have kicked his ass. As it was, in the 50s and 60s - protest would have found him in jail or hanging from a tree.

It is important to remember regarding race: my father was for all races. He wanted all people to succeed. However, it was particularly important for him, as a black man, to see his people succeed. He wanted them to learn from his hardships. He was sharing the pain of his youth with his people. When he wrote "Say it loud - I'm black and I'm proud," it was in an era when you didn't call somebody "black." They would've whooped your ass. You would have to fight them. He knew the people were ashamed of themselves for being black. All he was trying to do was to help black people be more proud of themselves as a people.

People didn't understand what he was really trying to say with that song. He wanted people to be proud of themselves as Americans first. He then wanted you to have pride in your race. He was criticized for that. He took a lot of slack from both black and white people. All he was ever trying to do is uplift people. He wanted to bring them out of the gutter. It was not a negative song toward any other people.

My father was an extraordinary human being. He was similar to Martin Luther King and Gandhi in many ways. He never received the Nobel Peace Prize, but he was able to command a crowd in the very same way - perhaps better. He was driven.

He would tell me all the time, "I don't understand why God uses me?"

People like that have a tendency to not see themselves as that kind of person. They don't see themselves as the person on top. They don't want to be someone like the president. He wanted to do his part - he didn't know why.

When he began stopping riots, he became a suspect of the FBI and the corrupt policies and practices of J. Edgar Hoover. Hoover attacked Martin Luther King hard. After King was assassinated, the most powerful black man in America was my father. Hoover and the FBI knew that if James Brown could stop a riot, he could start one. He and his music were more powerful than the president. The president used tanks to stop riots - my dad used song.

Tomi Rae confirmed, "Yes, the FBI began surveillance on James Brown after the Look magazine cover." My husband would always say – "Look up there (pointing to the sky). They got satellites following me. They got cameras in the house. They are always watching me."

Danny Ray said it best regarding my father's role with the Civil Rights movement:

"People like people. That's the business. The world had to change. If you treat people like people, it will be fine. If you separate them like that, nothing will grow. We are all God's children, man. You can't take time for that small minded thinking, you know. That will mess you up."

The Chase

December 15, 1988, The Godfather of Soul, Soul Brother No. 1, was convicted for failing to stop for a "blue light" and two additional counts of assault "of a high and aggravated nature." He went from soul-mate to cell-mate; South Carolina State felon number No. 155413.

Legend would have you believe that James Brown burst into an insurance meeting angrily firing his weapon over the unauthorized use of his bathroom. Like most legends, the story has a grain of truth that has now grown into a field of unsubstantiated factoids. My father's drug use during that time was undeniable, and unbelievable. He had two convictions of possession and use of PCP prior to "The Chase" during the same calendar year. Three arrests for possession and weapon's charges in a single year takes talent and stupidity. Most criminals, particularly drug users, will tell you it is not possible to count the number of times drugs were illegally used before they were finally caught. It takes effort and addiction to be repeatedly arrested.

My father denied allegations of drug use. That was one area where my father could not lie to me. I had been to the graduate school of drug use. I served time. Despite his protests, I knew exactly what was going on in my father's life. He said he was taking pain medication for his dental work. That may have been true. I know his teeth caused him great pain for most of his adult life. That perfect smile

252

came at a cost. Adrienne once said that my father had oral surgery three times in one month. She said that he was using several types of medicine. Critically, she also identified other symptoms: "He was agitated, could not sit still, and had difficulty concentrating."

These are not symptoms from heavy Lortab use. My father was using hard drugs during the 1980s, and it did not stop completely until his death. He spent the last week of his life high. Adrienne died with PCP coursing through her veins.

I am embarrassed to say, but sometimes I wonder if the Augusta police may have seen more of my dad than I did. Buddy Dallas was hired to keep my father out of legal trouble. That was a full-time job. Some police did work with Buddy and others to keep my father out of jail. Drugs, bad relationships, piles of cash and time away from the band invited constant trouble for my father.

Despite, or because of these challenges, he was a social and racial target for police in South Carolina. That was clear. A complaint was even made to the FBI chronicling the problems my father had with local police departments. No action was taken by the FBI or Department of Justice.

Donald Danner

It all took place on September 24th, 1988.
It began as a normal day. I was in charge of the drug abuse resistance education program, commonly called D.A.R.E. I

was asked by the Sheriff of Aiken County to provide a presentation to the folks at the Kroger market down on Martintown Road. I was only there for a few minutes when I heard the talk on the radio become very active. I thought, 'Maybe North Augusta has something going on.'

I left the store so I could hear more clearly. When I got outside, they said, "Chase in progress, coming in from Georgia to South Carolina."

I immediately asked the dispatcher, "What road are they coming in on?"

"They're coming off the interstate onto Martintown Road."

I told the people at the store, "Listen, I'll be right back. We've gotta hot chase going on."

I had no idea it was James Brown.

When I started traveling, I met what looked like some police officers escorting a celebrity. Mr. Brown had his big cowboy hat on and he's just waving, and he's got all of these police cars behind him. I said, 'Well, dog gone. They're not doing anything to stop it!'

The question of jurisdiction was an issue. I have county-wide jurisdiction and they have city-wide jurisdiction. They were now out of their jurisdiction. I didn't want to try and take over the incident until I was sure of what I was dealing with. I turned around and joined the James Brown parade.

On Georgia Avenue, the light turned red. Mr. Brown stopped for the light. He was being followed by police and obeying traffic signals. It was surreal.

I thought, 'One of these guys has gotta do something about this.' The 104.3 FM radio station was broadcasting details about the chase. We proceeded with the chase after the light changed. Something was not right. He was ignoring us. He heard all the sirens and saw the blue lights but I could not get him to pull over.

I passed the cars and moved right beside him. I was running the blue lights. All of the traffic was moving over. Me and Mr. Brown were within inches of each other and I looked directly into his eyes and said, "Pull over!" I pointed to the side of the road.

He pulled into a parking lot. He was traveling 35 mph, the speed limit. It was really more like an escort than a chase. He may have been speeding when he was traveling down I-20, but at this time, his speed was not excessive.

When we pulled into the vacated lot I jumped out of my vehicle and approached his truck. The vehicle was still running. Mr. Brown was distracted. I reached my left hand through the small front window and turned off the ignition. Everything was cool. We started to talk.

The North Augusta police department arrived quickly on the scene. These guys started jumping out of their cars and running toward the truck.

I said, "Hey man, everybody's cool. We got this under control." I needed them to back off.

While I'm communicating calm, one officer from North Augusta runs to the passenger side of the truck, takes his mag light out and busts the window. He startled Mr. Brown. You could see a look of terror in his eyes. James Brown was in danger.

Mr. Brown starts the ignition. I'm thinking to myself, 'Well, this looks like it's going to go south.' Now it had. Bullets started flying, and one went past my head - right by my ear.

I yelled "Woah!"

James Brown tells me, "I'm gettin' out of here!"

He puts the truck in gear and he's gone. I jump back. He's pshhhooo! Gone.

There was an officer clearly in front of the vehicle. He just stood there, wanting to be the hero or something. I don't know why he didn't move. He was a fool for standing there. If the suspect is cracked up - I'm not going to try and be no hero. You need to stay smart.

Suddenly, Mr. Brown leaves the scene. I'm on my radio to the Sheriff.

I said, "Man, things went south! These guys from the North Augusta police department are shooting at him. Mr. Brown has taken off again. It looks as if we're going to cross the bridge back into Augusta."

The Sheriff told me not to leave him.

The officers have shot up his tires and his entire truck. Tire fragments are blowing out all over the road. Curiously, he is driving steady. That took talent. He was not swerving all over the road. We were traveling about 15-20 mph. He started across the bridge and I thought for a moment he was taking us to his home in Beech Island. I think to myself, 'You know what, he may be going towards his house.' I'm thinking he's going toward home because that's where he lives.

I kept all the traffic behind me. He drove past a big school on the right and then turned left into a neighborhood. Unfortunately, the media was now broadcasting the chase and people were coming out of their homes to watch the Brown Parade fly by. Many people started to line the streets. I began to be concerned for their safety. The word was out: the Godfather of Soul is on the run.

By now, I am in Richmond County. I'm out of my jurisdiction. I'm out of my state.

The other police officers were somewhere behind me. I didn't really look back. I supposed those from North Augusta returned to their jurisdiction. I was completely focused on Mr. Brown.

We stopped in a neighborhood that was familiar to Mr. Brown. I believe he had an uncle that had worked for the Richmond County police department.

I quickly moved toward the truck and said, "Mr. Brown, I got you now."

He was defiant when he first stepped out of the truck and he saw so many people around him.

I told him, "Let's don't make anything between me and you."

It wasn't personal. I had a job to do. My job was to protect the citizens and protect Mr. Brown.

He looked up and I think he sees a couple of these Georgia state troopers and Richmond County deputies. He starts to make a break for it. I had to physically grab him. I actually put hands on him.

From that moment forward, he put up little resistance. I never thought my life was in danger or that he would try to harm me in any way. I did what I had to do to get him into the back seat of my car. I wanted to maintain jurisdiction. I know the Georgia trooper scared Mr. Brown - them's giants!

The troopers came over and I told them, "Listen guys, I don't know where we're going from here, but you all need to give me some space - I need some time."

They reminded me I was now in Georgia.

I said, "I know." I didn't want Mr. Brown transferred from one car to the other. I found out where we needed to take him.

I went back out to the road and there was a Richmond County officer. He said, "I'll transport him."

I said to the officer, "Well, I'm going to follow you. Wherever you go, I'm right behind you." I took Mr. Brown out of my car and transferred him into the custody of Richmond County. I walked into the police station with the old shotgun.

I called my sheriff and said, "We're at the Richmond County police department." He told me that he was working on Mr. Brown waiving his rights to extradition.

Mr. Brown had an ENORMOUS amount of cash in his possession and he was sweating profusely. He was perspiring so heavily they were not able to fingerprint him.

When I returned to our sheriff's office, the elected Sheriff and the lieutenant were waiting for me.

They said, "Danner, we need to see your gun." They wanted to make sure the gun had not been fired.

"Listen, my weapon never left my holster. Actually, they were shooting toward me while I was standing right there by the side of the truck! If anything, I could've shot back at them, but I didn't. I had complete focus on Mr. Brown."

I waited for things to cool down with Mr. Brown while he was being held in the cell.

I told the Sheriff, "I really need to go talk to Mr. Brown."

He asked why.

"Well, he needs to know that everybody that was out there was not against him. He needs to understand that I had a job to do, and that I spent more time protecting him than actually trying to make an arrest."

I was the arresting officer. No charges were filed against Mr. Brown from the Aiken County Sheriff's department. North Augusta was the agency that recommended certain charges be filed.

The Sheriff asked, "Danner, do you have any charges?"

I replied, "None of any relevancy. This should have been handled like a routine traffic stop. It turned into this big mess unnecessarily."

I am certain the North Augusta police department made recommendations. Had he been arrested by a different jurisdiction the outcome may have been very different.

This is important, when I had Mr. Brown pulled over the first time, these white cops started dropping all of their clips into Mr. Brown's truck. I know they tried to shoot out his tires but they almost shot me. I think if I had not been in the position next to the vehicle, The Godfather of Soul would have been killed that day. They would have shot him or blown the truck up. If a bullet went flying by my head, it must have gone by his as well. We were within inches of each other. They were amped up, but I can't believe they would miss so badly from short range.

I am particularly upset they didn't follow proper protocol and respect my authority as the first officer on the scene. I'll feel that way until the Good Lord calls me home. I was in charge; but I was black.

More than just the tires on the Ford truck were shot. They've still got the truck, don't they? (Brown had it restored) It had bullet holes all in the side of it, by the gas tank, doors, and everywhere else.

The justification for firing on the vehicle did not exist. What can I say? If my life or your life is in jeopardy, or there is a reasonable fear that the suspect is going to cause harm to someone, you can fire. But I had him stopped. He was fine. Shooting at the vehicle and breaking his window was a violation of policy.

Under normal circumstances, protocol requires you allow the officer on the scene to maintain control unless he needs to be relieved, or he turns over command of the situation. James Brown was not moving. His vehicle was turned off. I was within inches of the man. There was no struggle. I was interviewing him at the door. Everything was under control.

I never left the incident. I did not deviate from policy. I didn't lie for Mr. Brown then and I won't now. The prosecution knew my testimony was going to be very different from what they wanted to present to the court. The prosecution had me sequestered on the day of trial. I was waiting to testify, and then someone walked into the witness room.

They said, "They dropped you as a state witness."

I laughed - more of a smirk - and said, "Oh yeah, I'm sure they did." My testimony would have vindicated Mr. Brown.

There was a big tall attorney - big old boy. His name was Bill Weeks. Bill Weeks walks into the room. I've known Bill. He worked as a solicitor. We were friends. He said he represented Mr. Brown at the trial and all. I've known these cats for years as we've worked together in law enforcement.

Bill said, "Danner, listen up man. Guess what? State don't want you to testify. Would you testify for the defense?"

"I'll tell the story."

When I testified for the defense, oh man, you could see the heat in the courtroom. If these guys could pull out guns and shoot me - they would have. They must have been thinking - 'oh we got to get rid of this kid!'

They actually tried to have me terminated before trial. No grounds for termination existed. They wanted to scare me. I had what most would consider an impeccable record. I didn't have any flaws. I was a supervisor. A sergeant.

The sheriff, Carol Heath, was the one who told me what they were trying to do. He would not support them. I was assured that I wouldn't be terminated and he told me not to even worry about it.

I never went around Aiken County scared. I'm not that kind of person. I patrolled in North Augusta more frequently after the incident than I did prior. The police never bothered me. I have not had much contact with those officers. They became 'anti-social' toward me. They didn't want to come in contact with me or talk. Ironically, one of their officers joined the D.A.R.E program with me. We had to sit in classes together. I was waiting for homeboy to bring up something about the case. He wouldn't talk about it.

My story has not deviated from the beginning. I'm just as credible today as I was then. I have nothing to hide. I'm sorry for what happened to Mr. Brown. I wish I could've done a whole lot more. I've been persecuted for many other reasons, but it's always for doing the right thing. If you arrest people because of the color of their skin or their status in the community, you are not going to have a good reputation for being a great police officer.

I wanted to be a great police officer.

I cannot support the new movie coming out. I don't want to see it because it can't be factual - it can't be true. I've seen the previews - it is nowhere near the real thing. They got some cars as a road block that he busts through. If how they portrayed it was true, he would've never made it to Martintown Road.

Two years later I met Mr. Brown when he was on work release. I saw him at his office and approached him to introduce myself and shake his hand. He remembered who I was. He always remembered me.

He would stop and tell people, "You see that man? He saved my life." He'll tell you that in a heartbeat.

I will never forget the day I was front and center in the James Brown Parade.

***

Buddy Dallas clearly remembers 'The Chase.'

He stated, "Mr. Brown was convicted for failing to stop for a blue light in 1989 and went to prison for two years and three months. No one was harmed. There was no accident. Mr. Brown was scared. It was a fight or flight situation. He chose to leave the scene. Everybody in this part of the country knows who James Brown is. Where did the officers think he was going to hide? Where was he going to run? Why did he need to be chased? He was pulled over. He was in the custody of officer Danner. Everything was cool. The officers chased him from another jurisdiction. Obviously, they were excited. This, however, was an example of a black man being treated differently by white officers.

I had a plea deal worked out for Mr. Brown. He was going to serve 45 days. He would not take the plea deal. He felt it was wrong.

He said, "Mr. Dallas, I am entitled to an apology. For me to be chased down and shot at is an injustice."

Prior to the chase Mr. Brown was in his office. Inside the building there is a community space where an insurance seminar was taking place. Someone had entered Mr.

Brown's private restroom. Mr. Brown had an old shotgun that was used as a walking stick. It didn't even have the firing pin in it. Naturally nobody would know that, but it was inoperable.

He walked into the seminar and politely said, "Ladies and gentlemen I would appreciate being asked to use my restrooms."

Somebody called 911. Some lady pretended to faint. She filed a ridiculous lawsuit. We settled for a nominal amount. It was approximately $1000.

***

My father testified during the trial, "One police shot about eight times into the truck and then started to reload. I figure if a man shoots at me that many times and misses, then stops to reload, I'm gone. All I wanted to know, when he started to reload, was 'Would the truck start?' It cranked up and I took off."

That act of defiance saved his life.

In the FBI report, Adrienne indicated that 23 shots were fired - only 17 hit the truck. My father reported to the FBI 23 shots hit the truck including 2 that hit the gas tank.

A blood test administered by the police found PCP in his system.

The FBI report contains the following, "Mrs. Brown advised that she knows from reading that PCP can show up in the blood of a person who breathes the second-hand smoke of a person smoking PCP. She is sure her husband never used PCP, as he has always campaigned against the use of drugs in any form."

The story took a very interesting turn (if you believe Adrienne's FBI statement) that has not been widely reported. James and Adrienne Brown returned to their home around 10:00 p.m. My father was still in pain and feeling restless. When Adrienne awoke a couple of hours later my father was missing.

After looking for him on the property, she returned to their house and shortly received a call informing her that Brown had driven to Georgia War Veteran's Home in Augusta, where his father was hospitalized. Police arrested Brown for driving without a license, for speeding, and for yelling at some people, although he was just upset at seeing his father in the hospital. Brown was released from the Richmond County Jail that same day.

***

<u>Bill Weeks</u>

I first became acquainted with Mr. Brown many years ago, although we never formally met. I grew up in Beech Island three miles from his Beech Island residence. I used to pick plums, where his house was built. I wasn't a big James Brown fan. When I got out of law school in 1981, I came to the solicitor's office and started prosecuting cases. There were some domestic troubles between him and Adrienne.

I left the solicitors office on Labor Day of '85. I went to work for a firm that had represented James, like maybe filing for divorce, or defending a divorce action, or maybe a CDV (criminal domestic violence) in Magistrate's court. His cases had not come up to general session's court, the larger criminal court, for lack of a better description.

I had not met James. Mr. Brown was what he always wanted me to call him. We would hear people call him Mr. Brown. I had not met Mr. Brown until he walked into my office one day. My law partner who had represented him before was busy and couldn't see him.

He walked into our office and the secretary said, "Mr. James Brown is down here to see you."

And I said "Really?"

So he came up steps and all the employees were in awe and wanted to get autographs.

He was a delightful man. I mean it. That is the best description I could give. He was just delightful. He was fun to talk to. He was entertaining. He was funny. He was immaculately dressed in his style, whatever that was. His hair was done up and a scarf on. We got along great. I mean we were country. I grew up in Beech Island. He grew up in Barnwell. We could speak the same language. James Brown was kind of different in a way. He had been, I guess, groomed through the entertainment industry. I had never represented a "star" personality. When I started getting calls from People Magazine, and from his agents up

267

in New York, they were just as entertained by me as they were by James.

I had been a country prosecutor, a country lawyer. I still am. The first time I met him, he was charged with possession of PCP and for resisting arrest. That was a serious charge.

I represented him just three times, for three separate arrests. I might have filed a response of pleading or I might have actually filed a petition for divorce or separation at one time at his request. Primarily, I represented him for three different arrests, all within a year. As those arrests progressed, I got him out of jail on bond. They were staggered because they couldn't try him all at one time. The first one was possession of, I believe, PCP. The second time was PCP and resisting arrest. The third time was the North Augusta fiasco. That case made national and international news. That was the case where he was sentenced to prison.

James was a difficult client. He had an entourage, just to be candid, to pump him up and say, "Nothing is going to happen bad papa." But it was difficult to explain the realities of the world to Mr. Brown. I think my attorney's client privilege still stands even though he is dead. I am not going to really get into the things he told me privately, but I can certainly describe the setting of the criminal representation.

One interesting case started in Augusta, which is across the river from us, which means it is in another jurisdiction. James had an office over there in this little complex and they were having an insurance meeting in a large meeting room. Apparently James had been bent out of shape because they were coming up and using his rest room without asking permission. He went down there to the seminar. During discovery, we found that somebody was taping the lecture - we actually had a recording.

It was hilarious. James came in and you could hear him. It was his distinctive voice. You could hear him. He was saying something about, using the restroom: "Please don't do that." (Mr. Brown was particularly upset because he walked in on a woman using his restroom.) He had a shotgun with him. Why he took a shotgun in there I don't know, but the shotgun was a rugged old piece of crap. It could not fire. It was really just a walking stick.

He comes in and he sets the shotgun in the corner of the room and he is talking to whoever is moderating the thing and saying, "Don't use my bathroom blah, blah, blah."

He gets ready to leave and you hear a voice from the audience saying, "Mr. Brown. Don't forget your gun." It was a polite tone. It was comical - but somebody thought it was serious enough to call the Richmond County Sheriff's Department (Augusta, Georgia). Richmond County Sheriff's department is responding and James takes that time to leave. Well, he left and actually traveled down to I-20.

The tape gave an indication that James Brown was "very spirited." I think during this period of time, that was James's whole problem. He was constantly using drugs. Of course, the other problem was Adrienne. He was addicted to using PCP - hard drugs.

He jumps in his Ford truck. That would have made a great commercial. He is traveling down Interstate 20 and all of Richmond County Police are behind him. They know who he is. So they are not really trying to run him off the road. They are really just following him and clearing the way down the road.

As you cross the river, you would be traveling East on I-20 and then enter North Augusta, South Carolina. Police are heading that way to intercept him on I-20 but he didn't go I-20. He pulled off the freeway on a street called Martintown Road. They are turning around and James goes blasting by. Their testimony was that he was speeding. Mr. Brown was driving excessively fast and they put the "blue lights" and siren on him. That began the chase. I estimate the speed was around 80 mph.

The officers testified that they pursued him between two and three miles. Behind him is Officer Donald Danner. He caught up to Mr. Brown and pulled his vehicle beside James. He is a black officer. He was not going to pull over for the others chasing him. He did not know if they were black, white, green, or yellow. When Donald pulled alongside, he directed Mr. Brown to an intersection that had an abandoned service station.

Then officers testified that when he cleared Georgia Avenue, a major intersection between Martintown and Georgia Ave., his truck left the road. They estimated between five and eight feet. That was just unbelievable. It was an obvious gross exaggeration.

That is what the testimony was and that is what I knew their testimony was going to be. These are the challenges I had to contend with.

All of the officers gather around the truck. James is in the truck and Donald has it stopped. I think he is outside of his car, but North Augusta pulls in there and I remember three of the officers.

They are all white. They were all veterans of the force.

They have been around and are not bad officers. I mean, I don't want to say they were bad. They were good. But by the time they got him pulled over they were pretty hyped. This is a chase through downtown North Augusta at pretty high speeds. They had heard the information that Mr. Brown had a gun and had threatened a bunch of people. This was not an unreasonable response.

This was a felony situation. They got out with their weapons drawn.

James won't go anywhere at that point in time. He has a gun in his truck. Billy Lucky approaches the truck and smashes in the window and grabs the shotgun which is just lying on the seat. Like I said, it's a piece of shit.

It wouldn't operate. It is like the kind of guns we see "dopers" carrying around. Billy Lucky snatches it out of the truck and starts yelling for Brown to get out. James, to his reasonable credit, kind of freaks out at that point and attempts to pull away and leave. Well, they opened fire on his tires. They are on either side of the car shooting those front tires. It's a miracle nobody got killed. They were not trying to kill James.

One of them - and I gave him hell during closing arguments - he's a great guy, a friend of mine and will probably always have a little animosity toward me after a closing argument. I call him Captain Lucky for a reason. He reloaded his gun, he emptied another clip. He shot 16 times at those tires.

I don't know the total amount of rounds that were fired, but they shot up those tires. I think, they really all expected them to go 'poof, and blow, but they don't. You shoot a hole in a tire. It's a hole in a tire. It's going to let out air. It's not going to blow up like on TV unless you shoot it with a bazooka. But James gets away and they say they had to jump out of the way. So they charged him with trying to run over them, which was an assault with intent to kill charge. This was a stumbling block in trying to get the case resolved.

The officers got out of the way and James travels on what we call Aiken-Augusta Highway - or Highway 1. At this time all of his tires are flat, I think, and he was literally riding on the rims. He crosses the Savannah River and back into Georgia. He makes a big loop.

They never try to stop the vehicle. They didn't try to run him off the road. He pulled into the yard and they're all on top of him. Richmond County has come back into the fold. It was a hell of a Ford commercial.

I am shocked nobody was hit by a stray bullet, or it didn't kill somebody a mile away. It's always been amazing to me.

I don't think James was being unreasonable, just to be candid. I don't know. I don't know what had him agitated that particular day. I never really knew. But the problem with the case was he'd just been put on probation for the other two PCP cases, and was now charged with attempting to assault police officers. At the time it was called 'assault with intent to kill.' Two counts for the two police officers that said they had to get out of the way. And they probably did have to get out of the way, but that is because they were in the way. He was also charged with failure to stop for a blue light and believe it or not, at that time, in that era, failure to stop for a blue light in South Carolina could carry up to ten years.

The judge had discretion when it came to sentencing. They offered 18 months. You go to jail for 18 months on plea. Mr. Brown did not want to accept.

He went and got sentenced in Georgia. Honestly, I don't remember what his sentence was in Georgia. I was thinking it was more like fines or 30 days...I believe he paid the fine in Georgia and was done with it.

During the trial in South Carolina we have circuit judges that move from county to county. The judge presiding over this case was from a neighboring circuit. His name was Hubert Long.

Judge Long said to us that he was called to come to Aiken to hear this case about some singer that he didn't know. Judge Long was old at the time. He was older than James by 15 years. He was colorful, loud, and big.

Oh Lord. Every time Judge Long appeared, he told the court jokes about his goats and his garden, but it was not entertaining, more like stressful. He was, though, a tremendously nice judge to me and the other lawyers. He'd never been to Aiken while I had been a prosecutor. It was my first experience with him, and he was respectful and robust and he treated us nice.

It was not like it would be today. There might have been a newspaper reporter or two outside. CNN wasn't down there. It was less popular locally than it was in New York City. It was a classic situation for James Brown. It's like politics; politicians can do tremendously well nationally and not get a vote in their home town. Well, James was that way.

James was on probation for one of his arrests. I pushed hard for probation. As a condition of probation he would perform a concert. There was a circuit judge out of Greenwood named Jim Moore. He was also a delightful man. This was Mr. Brown's second arrest within the year for PCP and he was going to jail. We talked the judge into giving him probation.

I think the entourage came up with that idea. Buddy Dallas was a lawyer in Thompson that hatched the idea. The judge agreed, but it was not warmly received. I had to get the prosecutor to agree first - but the prosecutor was my former boss so he was pretty flexible.

Mr. Brown was not being prosecuted for the color of his skin. He was being prosecuted because he wouldn't stop being arrested!

Interestingly, Mr. Brown would never admit to me that he was involved with drugs or PCP. He was adamant that he'd never taken anything. He was drug free. He never drank, didn't smoke - didn't do anything entertainers did. Then he was repeatedly arrested for possession.

The trial lasted about three and a half or four days. I'm not sure why it took that long, because it was not a complex trial with numerous accounts. I think it probably lasted a day longer than it should have because the judge talked all the time. The judge has since died.

Truly, in 1989, he was not a bad judge to be in front of. He did however sentence Mr. Brown to six and one half years. At the time, it was a longer sentence than any similar felony stop I had ever witnessed. Our moral victory was that he was not convicted with assault with intent to kill but rather assault of a high and aggravated nature. It was just a small moral victory, however, because both of them carried the same sentence - up to ten years max.

I never got the impression that James was ever upset at me, or anybody associated with the trail for that matter.

I've only seen Mr. Brown a few times after his incarceration. He was just as pleasant as ever. He was way more respectful than he needed to be. He'd call me Mr. Weeks - he wouldn't call me Bill. He liked to be called Mr. Brown and he'd call me Mr. Weeks. That was just the way he was.

It was not a complicated case, truly. I had a number of police officers testifying. It was interesting; we received phone calls during the trial from people who had witnessed the chase. Most of them confirmed that James was not trying to run over any of the officers. All of the officers in the case I knew would talk to me without hesitating. I knew what they were going to say and I'd tell James what they were going to say.

I wish the police would have just followed him to wherever he was going, but I guess that was really not an option for them. They didn't know if he was on PCP or if the gun was going to be used as a weapon. The only issue I had was the charge of assault against him. That is, from my stand point, overkill. That is probably the wrong term but he wasn't trying to kill anybody. He was just trying to get away. There was too much pressure from the police to let that go.

Prosecutors are elected here in Aiken. James had his share of breaks from the prosecutor. He was not inclined to give him much of a break - he had plenty of breaks previously.

I gave a television interview with one of the TV stations from up North several years after the case. I remember telling them something I repeatedly told Mr. Brown: "James, you're not going to have a jury of 12 African American entertainers. You're going to have a jury of 12 people from Aiken County. They may know who you are, they probably would've listened to some of your records, but they're not going to care who you are. If these people get up there and testify that you were driving 80-90 miles an hour through their town they're going to convict you for failure to stop for a blue light."

The law in this state was, and still is, you can testify you didn't see a blue light. If the weather was such that a normal person would've seen it, that's enough to convict. This is important. He felt like if he was convicted, there would be riots in the streets of Augusta. A lot of what I would hear from James was historical stuff about him

277

speaking to the crowds in Augusta during the 1960s when they were rioting in the streets. He told the people to "be cool." I've heard all his stories before.

He would come to me and say, "There'd be riots if I get convicted." He felt like he was the next Nelson Mandela. He wanted to be idolized – not just in his world, but mine.

He said he was another Nelson Mandela.

I told him, "Mr. Brown, there may be a letter to the editor if you get convicted, but there ain't going to be no rioting in the streets, and you're going to jail. And that's not going to be good."

He responded, "Well if that happens, it happens."

I don't remember seeing much of Adrienne during the trial. I don't know what their relationship was at the time.

He was sentenced to State Park - a minimum security facility. I would go to see him because I had to do submit an appeal to the Supreme Court. The appeal had little validity. He wanted me to do it. My argument was very poor and it would have made bad law.

Oh hell, Al Sharpton called me on the phone, or somebody reporting to be Al Sharpton, called and talked about coming to Aiken. He may have even had a press conference on the courthouse steps. If he was a preacher, his language to me on the phone was horrendous. He said that James Brown had been railroaded by the people of Aiken because he was a black man.

There's a great video clip of me going to get him out of Aiken County Detention Center one morning after he was arrested for one of the PCP events. His hair was all over the damn place. We get in my truck. I had fishing poles hanging out the back. I pulled out and all of the press portrayed the scene as: "Country come to Town."

My wife gave me hell about Mr. Brown's hair.

I told her, "I didn't have a hairdresser in jail."

Of course, that was the first question James asked, "Does anybody here dig my hair?"

I said, "Mr. Brown let's just be quiet and get you out of here."

I never saw James where I thought he was anything other than the same man the first time I met him. Honestly, I didn't go to his house and socialize or go on trips with him.

Every now and then he'd say, "I want you to go to Italy with me."

I would respond, "Mr. Brown, I'm from Aiken, I'm not going to Italy, I appreciate it but I'm not doing that."

He was just so vivacious. That is the only way I ever saw him. Now, honestly, that vivaciousness could've been because he was high as a kite. I've told people for years that if James Brown walked into a room full of people that were the worst bigots in the world they would love him. Hell, Strom Thurman loved James Brown.

I would visit Mr. Brown in prison.

He would say to me, "Mr. Weeks, thank you so much! I needed the rest."

I responded, "Man I didn't give you this 24 months you're fixing to serve."

I don't regret any of my representation of James Brown. He was a character; one of the great characters of my career. He was such a nice guy - he just he wasn't real good with the marital relationship thing and that led to malicious behavior.

***

James Brown was found guilty and sentenced to six years in prison. Adrienne complained to the FBI that a 19 year old white man had received six months on a second offense of the same kind.

Additionally, on January 23, 1989, my father went to trial in Richmond County, Georgia on eleven traffic violations resulting from the same incident at the War Veterans' Home. Susie Brown was present during that trial. She looked at him with tears in her eyes and made the sign of the Cross with her index finger. The judge sentenced Brown to a six-year prison term, to run concurrent with the South Carolina sentence. My father told the FBI that he pled guilty on the advice of his attorney and that he didn't even know what the charges were in Georgia.

My father made an interesting statement to the FBI. He said that he feared a break-in at his office was taking place. He did have a safe in his office on the other side of the bathroom wall. He returned to the truck and got his shotgun and took it back to the office. When he walked into the insurance seminar he placed the shotgun in the corner of the room. He asked that the keys to his private bathroom be returned and then he locked the bathroom door. That was his explanation for the shotgun.

Dad was angry that people abandoned him while he was in prison. Family and entertainers did not come to visit. Please add my name to the list. I returned home to New Jersey. I had a family that I needed to provide for.

Bobby Byrd, my father's lifelong friend rhetorically asked, "Where are his friends?...They're as far away as they can get."

While Adrienne came to visit my father - others came to visit Adrienne. It is common knowledge among many that a close associate of my father "visited" Adrienne every time he came to town. Unfortunately, Adrienne talked and Adrienne made a video tape. Unsubstantiated rumors exist about other lovers. Adrienne had very expensive habits and she needed money while my father was in prison. There were times where she told others she had no food in the home. She was desperate. She needed compensation for her services. Undoubtedly, she missed my father and she missed his money.

Buddy Dallas said it more succinctly: "Adrienne Brown was a real addict and she hated Mr. Brown. Whatever propensity Mr. Brown had - she exacerbated all of the problems. She would take cookies into the prison - they were laced with drugs. I believe she convinced herself that Mr. Brown was far worse of a man than he really was. I know she falsified reports against him."

I have often wondered why my father never confronted the man who was sleeping with his wife. I believe that such a confrontation would be a sign of his weakness. Why would the wife of James Brown stray if he was taking care of her? An affair would be a commentary on his sexual prowess. He had spent 40 years building a reputation of unsurpassed sexual prowess. He would not allow a high-profile tryst to ruin his reputation. He was the Sex Machine.

His drug induced comments to Sonya on CNN (April 4, 1988) provide context: "...I make love good...AAAAHHHHHH!"

My father had similar ideas regarding his band and his employees. If his band or office employees ever publicly displayed financial need, he believed it was a poor reflection on him as an employer. That idea was very important to him. Similarly, if he acknowledged a drug problem he would admit to physical or moral weakness. Of course, recognition is the first step in every recovery program. Rigid denial is simply a symptom of addiction that continues the persistent problems in their lives.

My father said a few interesting things surrounding the trial: "I've been in slavery all my life, ain't nothing new. It just means I don't have to answer a whole lot of phone calls. Ain't nothing changed for me but the address."

The idea of my father as a slave is both fascinating and sad. Clearly he felt a heightened level of oppression for the color of his skin. This case was no exception. He also was a slave to those he provided for. That was a burden he assumed - but it was a burden nonetheless. The people that he provided financial assistance to extended far beyond his entourage, his employees, his wife, her family, and his multiple mistresses. The majority of requests were from desperate souls who petitioned the Godfather of Soul for assistance each and every week. By the hundreds, these people appeared at his door with their hands out.

He was also tired. Everyone knew the number of shows and the intensity of his performance was unequaled in the entertainment industry. This was a time to repair and restore his mind and body. He did take advantage of the time during his incarceration.

After serving more than two years, Buddy Dallas brought my father before the South Carolina Board of Paroles and Pardons.

He began his remarks, "It is my distinct pleasure to introduce you to James Brown; a man known locally, nationally, and internationally."

My father also had the legal help of Reginald Simmons. Reggie provided legal services to my father simply as a professional courtesy. My father was both touched and indebted. Reggie remained close to my father for years. Twenty minutes after the proceedings began, the board paroled my father.

The first night he came out of prison he played a concert for $1 million. It was a Pay-per-view production by the boxing promoter Butch Lewis. The money was paid prior to the concert. His career and net worth soared after that performance.

Illusions

My father used to say, "We are in business; show business." The entertainment industry is about creating and maintaining illusions for the purpose of captivating an audience. What you believe to be true - rarely is. Fame doesn't create confidence; fame is the footing for self-doubt. The more you crave fame for fames sake, the easier it becomes to walk away from the person you wanted to become.

Whether or not you believe many in this industry have "sold their soul" may not be the point. In truth, many in the entertainment industry simply gave it away.

The following stories are about the "industry" - the "business" of illusion and control.

***

Black Caesar, written and directed by Larry Cohen, was a blaxploitation fictional film. The anti-hero, Tomi Gibbs, rises from social obscurity to control the streets of Harlem as the head of an organized crime syndicate. The film was released in 1973, one year after another Mafia movie, The Godfather.

Charles Bobbit brought the soundtrack deal to my father.

He is clear. "James Brown never saw the movie until the premier. He never even talked to Larry."

285

Yet, my father felt Black Caesar was his life's story. There are some fascinating parallels. The parallels are not necessarily literal in all cases. However, the coincidences are startling. The story is more of a metaphor for my father's life. Perhaps this is what my father saw.

Consider:

Tomi Gibbs was working to raise money to help his struggling family. He did so by shining shoes.

Tomi is on the wrong side of police corruption and spends several years in a juvenile correctional facility.

Tomi's estranged parent re-enters his life.

Tomi's mother passes. "Although Susie would not die for years, the song written for this scene is one of the most beautiful songs ever composed by James Brown; Mama's Dead. My father wept when he recorded this track at home in Augusta. The song has a haunting melody saturated with personal pain. The wound inflicted by his mother was so deep and infected with poverty, prostitution and personal loneliness that my father remained emotionally scarred until death. Re-released today, I believe the song would quickly rise on the charts."

Mama's Dead contains the following lyrics:
No one to cry, no one to sit by the bed side
No one to watch the light in my window
No one, no one to come in
Come in and pull the cover over my head at night
No one to say, 'son, everything will be alright.'

Tomi, now Black Caesar, returns to his home after his mother's funeral to be intimately held in the sweet charms of a married woman. Tomi angrily rejects her extramarital advances.

Black Caesar is told, by this unfaithful spouse, that his wife is sleeping with another man - one of his closest confidants.

Black Caesar's wife seduces and betrays him to gain access to his personal fortune.

Black Caesar and his unfaithful friend (the man sleeping with his wife) are reunited in the final scenes.

Black Caesar has a long-time friend and confidant that is a man of the cloth. He accompanies Tomi as he builds his dark empire.

Finally, Black Caesar was killed by those who wanted to take his empire.

Fred Wesley, James Brown's band director in '73, was masterful in filling in whatever holes my dad may have left in the score. Mr. Bobbit was listed as a co-writer for several of the songs. Bobbit admits that while he may have provided James Brown with certain ideas or lyrics, the designation was simply a way to make sure he was properly compensated for his critical role in bringing my father the contract.

Bobbit was not finished. The movie inspired an idea for branding James Brown. Given the popularity of the Godfather in 1972 and Black Caesar in 1973, Bobbit wanted to combine the two central themes of each movie and cast my father as The Godfather of Soul. The clever title was not given without consequence.

My father took the title Godfather seriously. It became his identity. I don't know exactly why. He would talk to me privately about corruption in the music and entertainment industry. "You don't understand how bad this business can be."

I know my father was involved with corrupt people and corrupt organizations. The Godfather lived in a world of creating and maintaining illusions.

Teddy was my father's favorite son. Of course it pains me to say that - but it is the truth. Teddy had talent, charisma, and a good mind. His fuse might have been short - all the Brown boys had short fuses when they were young - but man could Teddy dance and sing. He was the heir apparent to James Brown.

My father told me that Teddy was executed in the left temple. He believed the execution was a personal attack due to his business dealings. "They" were trying to get to my father. "They" do so by killing you or your firstborn. "They" killed my father's favorite son in an effort to keep my father in line.

Teddy did not die in a car accident, he was murdered. It was not car crash, he was killed. It was a sacrifice. This is a true story. He was not killed in a car accident, he was shot.

288

Perhaps the person who suffered most from the death of my brother Teddy is my brother Terry. He was the next oldest. He thought his life was in jeopardy as well. That is heavy. If you look at what happened, there was a bullet hole on the left side of his head; right in the temple. That's how they did him. They killed him first and then they pushed the car down the embankment.

Terry told me that Teddy was run off the road. Teddy got out of the car and confronted the reckless driver. They executed him right then and there.

My father knew; he absolutely knew. He thought "they" were going kill all the children. That is why he kept us at a distance. My father was a black man with significant power. Maintaining that amount of power was not acceptable in our country during that time.

I don't have the physical evidence to prove my brother was executed the way my father told me. I do know my father believed it and it deeply impacted his behavior toward me and others. While the story does seem unbelievable, when you are playing the game, any game, with tens of millions - now hundreds of millions - of dollars on the table, people are always hurt while others are simply removed. Take an inventory of the people in politics and the entertainment industry that were assassinated, murdered, or died covered in a shroud of suspicious circumstances from the 60s forward. Make the list - you will see.

There are some terrible things in this business. My father would say to me, "They don't want you to do that."

I would ask him, "Who is THEY? Who in the hell are THEY?"

There are things you just don't see in life until you get to the very top. Then it's too late to take a step back. It's intense.

As I got older and more into the industry, I started understanding those very same things for myself. He told me that I had a gift for music. I could be successful without him. He told me to stay away from the major record labels. He wanted me to be independent. He didn't want me to be beholden to people who could do me harm.

My father told Tomi Rae the same story.

She said, "James Brown said his son Teddy was definitely murdered for being with white women in the car when they took the trip to Toronto. There was evidence they had attacked the black men in the car and left the white women alone. When you looked at the accident and the dead bodies there was evidence. The white women were not touched, or something to that effect. He told me somebody had come and bashed their heads in after the fact. That is what he believed. That is what tore him apart. He loved Teddy."

Charles Bobbit disagrees. Bobbit was one of the last people to see Teddy.

Bobbit said, "He came to see me at the Americana hotel. He stopped by to tell me he was going to Canada to get a job. I was the last person to see him other than those who were in the car. I think I gave him some money - although I am not quite sure.

Mr. Brown called me and told me his son had been in a car accident. I started to investigate. I timed the accident. I went to the scene of the accident and then calculated the speed he was traveling. I considered the time they left New York City until the accident they had to average more than 65 mph. They were flying, when you consider the traffic they would have faced to get out of the city. They were in a small compact car. Apparently, they fell asleep while driving. I never heard anything about a bullet in the side of the head. I don't believe that. Mr. Brown has said, "I wonder if he was murdered - or was he alright?" The undertaker never said that Teddy had been shot or stabbed. That would have been news.

I don't believe Charles Bobbit is correct. I have a hard time accepting a young 19 year old man with a car full of people would fall asleep at the wheel within 2 hours of leaving New York City.

My father told the same story to David Cannon and several others in the office. Without an autopsy nobody will know the truth. Why would my father tell that story to so many?

My father had a thing about keeping his enemies close to him. He'd say he would keep his friends close, but his enemies closer. My father had a lot of gangsters around him during his early career. They were pimps and number runners.

He had a number of people that would tell him "yes" to anything he asked. Uncle Henry Stallings, who he grew up with, was not a "yes" man. He would tell him not to believe that shit. Those people who were "yes" men could never stay around long. Henry Stallings kept things balanced. Danny Ray was also a very good friend.

My daddy used to say to me, "Son, you don't really know who I am."

It would make me upset when he would say, "What do you mean - I don't know you?"

But, the fact is, I didn't know him. I didn't really get to know my father until we started traveling around the world together. I was with him more than I was with my own children - my own family. You really get to know a man when you travel with him for eight years.

***

My father was offered millions of dollars to convert to Islam. President Bongo of the nation of Gabon in West Africa made repeated gestures to solicit my father's international celebrity status and become a Muslim. My father would have no part in that.

In 1967 the president of Gabon promoted Bongo to vice president. The President was dead within a year and Bongo began his 45-year reign of corruption. I apologize to the dead, but the President of Gabon was an evil man. He was bad news.

He was physically small with a Napoleon complex. He believed everything in the nation of Gabon belonged to him. Bongo pillaged the nation's wealth. The dictator of an oil-rich nation made Bongo worth hundreds of millions of dollars. He allowed the citizens of Gabon to have just enough money to avoid insurrection. He paid off political opponents, bought elections, and his enemies mysteriously disappeared.

Bongo converted to Islam in 1973. It is uncertain exactly when the first offer occurred. David Cannon made it clear that multiple offers were made; the most recent was in June or July of 2006. The amount offered increased from one million dollars to twelve million dollars over time. It is unknown if Gabon made similar offers to others. Habits die hard. Bongo made a career of purchasing loyalty. If he was willing to buy the celebrity of my father - did he make other offers of a similar nature?

David Cannon, Buddy Dallas, Danny Ray and Tomi Rae have all corroborated the story.

Buddy Dallas said, "Mr. Brown was a patriot. He loved this country. He loved this country despite the way he was treated. I remember one trip he had to the Middle East. He told me the following story. 'Mr. Dallas, I was offered $1 million to become a Muslim. Do you know what I told them Mr. Dallas? While I mean no disrespect to your God, the God that brought me into this world will be the same God that takes me home. All they asked me to do is to say publicly that I was a Muslim. I would not do it.'"

Danny Ray tells the same story, "We performed in a lot of Muslim countries. James Brown was offered millions of dollars to convert to Islam. But he wasn't going to go that way. That's not who he was. Now, they tried, but he wasn't going to change. No way.

Tomi Rae said, "Brown told the story often. It is true. James Brown was offered millions of dollars to convert to Islam by President Omar Bongo of Gabon. This happened several times throughout his life. The first time it happened all of the money was sitting there on the table. James simply walked out of the room. He said he was afraid he was going to get shot. The first time the money was lying right on the table and when he walked out he wasn't sure if he was going to get out of there alive. He told them he was not going to convert. He came into the world with his god and hoped to leave with the very same god. This was a story that I heard him tell more than once. People on the "inside" knew the truth."

David Cannon remembers the story clearly: "I do know James Brown was offered $12 million by a country in the Middle East if he would convert to Islam and go public with his conversion. The final time he was offered money to convert was in June or July of 2006. He said he would never do that. He would talk more to Mr. Bobbit about his religious ideas as well as many of the preachers in town he was close to. He would often give the preachers around town thousands of dollars when he attended their Sunday services."

The connection to Gabon and President Bongo was Charles Bobbit. Others have told the story of how he pocketed money that belonged to my father and left to serve as an advisor to President Bongo. I don't know the truth of the story. That story belongs to Bobbit and my father. What I do know is Bobbit provided a pipeline for Gabon to my father and he brought Michael Jackson to Africa as well. The stories that come out of Gabon are dark, very dark, and they should be told by others.

***

February 15, 1978 was one of the greatest upsets in sports history. Leon Spinks won the undisputed heavyweight championship of the world in a 15-round split decision. Most everyone on the planet was shocked at the result; everyone except for the man in the ring, Muhammad Ali.

Hollie Farris

I remember spending time with Muhammad Ali. We were playing in Vegas. Ali was fighting Leon Spinks for the first time. He invited us to his suite after a sparring session. We spent two or three hours talking with him. That was amazing!

I will never forget what he first said to me when we were introduced.

Someone said, "Muhammad, this is Mr. Hollie Farris. He plays trumpet with Mr. James Brown."

He smiled, took me by the hand and said, "Have they made a nigger out of you yet?"

I was speechless! That was just his sense of humor. He was funny. He was so sharp and really soft-spoken. He's not loud and boisterous as you see before his fights. He was such a nice man.

Muhammad Ali was not full of himself. He was a great guy. He was so smart. We were watching him train and we talked to him. We would say, "Muhammad you are going to destroy Spinks!"

He stopped us, and turned around. He looked at us and said, "What if I lost? What if I lost and there was a rematch? What if I lost and then had a HUGE rematch and I became the first heavyweight champion of the world to win the title three times! It would be bigger than ever!"

That is exactly what happened. I believe he lost on purpose. As you know, the next time they fought, he beat him. I know it's true. This is exactly what he said. "I will win my title back for the third time."

That had never happened before. That is exactly what he did. He lost his title to Spinks and won it back for the third time. He planned it!

He was a very smart man. He was smarter than people gave him credit for. I was impressed. It happens in sports all the time if you think about it. That is one of the best sports stories of all time. He planned it out the whole time.

He said, "But what if?"

We kept telling him, "You are going to beat him so bad. You are going to destroy Spinks."

He would always reply, "What if I lost?"

I didn't understand what he was doing at the time. It hit me a couple years later after I had time to think about it. He told us exactly what he was going to do.

James Brown was not with us when we were with Muhammad Ali. I suspect that is why we got to talk to Muhammad Ali. Mr. Brown would have dominated the entire room. He had so much charisma. It would've been an entirely different conversation if James were there.

Sports Illustrated quoted Muhammad Ali on February 27, 1978: "Don't call me champ - he's the champ. You don't have to call me champ to be my friend. I shall return. I'll let him hold the title a few months and enjoy it. Then I shall return."

Ali may have been the only person that knew he was going to lose. I doubt it - but if there were others it would have been a very, very small circle.

Spinks was stripped of his WBC title for refusing to take on the number one ranked challenger Ken Norton. The Spinks-Ali rematch would be at the Louisiana Superdome. 63,000 fans eagerly waited to see the rematch. Little more than 5,000 attended the first fight at the Hilton in Las Vegas.

In May of 2014, Leon Spinks answered the question to Livefight.com: "I just went for gold and took the bigger money fight. We'll never know about me and Kenny, but I think I could have beaten him. It's just Ali was the bigger fight at that stage."

Ali said before the fight, "I know this will be my last fight. I'll be three times champion."

Angelo Dundee, his famous trainer said, "What I'm counting on is how badly he wants to win it for the third time - to be the only man to ever do it. He has a sense of history. And, let's face it, Ali is not like other men."

After the fight, Ali reminded his audience that this was a difficult bout. Tragically it was his final competitive fight. "I killed myself to get ready for Spinks. I suffered and sacrificed more than I ever did. There's nothing left for me to gain by fighting."

Muhammad Ali sent an official letter of retirement to the WBA in June of 1979. Ali held boxing promoter Bob Arum hostage, demanding $1,000,000 be paid in ransom. The AP reported that the two parties settled on $300,000.

Arum said, "We knew Muhammad Ali was going to retire, but as long as he delayed, I couldn't make definite plans."

Coincidentally, Spinks' promoter was Butch Lewis, the same man who would pay my father $1,000,000 to perform in concert after he was released from prison.

The most important idea to keep in mind, whether it is in politics or entertainment - follow the money. Ali was always the smartest man in the room. He was playing three dimensional chess while others were trying to figure out their first move on the checkerboard.

***

Respect was critical for my father. The stories of James Brown insisting people use formal titles such as Mr. or Mrs. are widely known. What is not widely known is the respect he demanded from his peers in the entertainment industry. Generally, people were gracious. However, one TV and film star inadvertently angered my father.

Buddy Dallas

I will never forget the time in the Beverly Hills Hilton Hotel when Mr. Brown was performing. He was at the Forum in Los Angeles if I remember correctly. Bill Cosby was also in the hotel. Bill Cosby sends to Mr. Brown's suite a pot of collard greens. I am telling you that I had to restrain Mr. Brown. He wanted to go down and beat the hell out of Bill Cosby - my words, not his. He felt as though Mr. Cosby had disrespected him.

That highlights the point I am trying to make. Mr. Brown was not accepted by educated, uppity, snooty, arrogant, elite people in the black community. Mr. Brown was viewed as being crass or uncouth. The truth is, Mr. Brown had more knowledge, talent, and experience in his little finger than they had in their entire body.

Many people might use a noun, a pronoun, a verb or adjective properly. Brown may use the same word inappropriately in some sentences. Mr. Brown may not have known what the Pythagorean Theorem was. However, he had a mind that was sharper than anyone's in the room. If you pushed him very hard at all, he would whip your ass and he wouldn't take but a moment to do it.

***

Politics

My father loved current events and politics. His relationship with the White House began with Lyndon Johnson and continued with Vice President Hubert Humphrey in the 1960s. His "turncoat" support of Nixon was met with disdain among the black community for obvious reasons. His affection for President Nixon seems misguided today - it was not then. Access to the White House ended with a "gold card" or direct line to the Oval Office of President George W. Bush. Access to the White

300

House and other political leaders was not enjoyed by Dr. Martin Luther King.

Brown often began his day writing presidents, senators, or congressmen, depending on what issue piqued his interest (and depending how high he was later in life). He called their offices regularly.

He was thrilled the day President Bill Clinton called him. He loved Bill Clinton, but was disappointed when the news broke concerning the Monica Lewinsky affair. Irony, or hypocrisy?

The Oval Office embodied a sense of dignity and historical significance that was not appropriate for extramarital activity. Such license belonged to the entertainment industry - not to the President of the United States. What most people don't understand about James Brown is that he deeply loved his country. He had Republican sympathies, but wanted to support whoever held the office. The fate of the nation was more important than the fate of one man.

My father was invited to perform for the Nixon inauguration in January of 1969. Previously, Nixon had underhandedly referred to my father's support. He was misleading the black population regarding my father's formal or informal support. This was the game my father was playing. He was doing to both political parties the very same thing he had done to the band, his employees, his wives, and lovers. He was pitting them against each other for his benefit.

James Brown was sly as a fox. His gift may not have been political speech, but he was unequaled in manipulating people. The Democrats held the purse strings during the Nixon administration, but Nixon could direct funds as they became available. Brown needed funds focused on black causes and black educational infrastructure. Nixon furthered black causes more than previous Democratic presidents. Republicans were so thrilled that the most high-profile black man in America would join their political ranks, they would bend over backwards to keep him in their fold.

Conversely, the Democratic Party now needed to up their game. If James Brown was jumping ship - who would follow? They needed to take care of their constituents. The party's commitment to black causes needed to increase to prevent an exodus of voters.

Who won this game? Illusion and control. For James Brown, this was nothing more than a tactic to benefit his people. He could not publicly sell the idea to his fans - he had to remain quiet to complete his conquest. Political parties crave celebrity. He used this craving against both political parties. Politics is not just about hope and change; the game is also motivated by fear and loss.

I Feel Good

I have taken you Inside the Godfather in a way that few, if any, have been able. I am grateful for those who have shared their stories. Thank you.

This final chapter includes some of my fondest memories of James Brown. They are not in any particular order. These are reflections of people, places, and events that would have him say, "Wo! I feel good."

The most important idea I want you to understand about my father was something he often said: "When God resurrects you - you got to resurrect others."

In 1987, my father announced his intention to give the children of Georgia and South Carolina most of his wealth. He established a trust fund for the poor and needy children to receive funds for their education. It was estimated the trust fund would have been worth $100,000,000. If you knew my father at all, he never wanted any child to suffer as he did. Smiles he witnessed on their faces brought a sense of pride that was only equaled by the joy he felt performing.

Similarly, the practice of giving away as many as a thousand turkeys at Thanksgiving was one of the highlights of his year. He began the day with a public prayer, sang with a gospel choir, and shook the hands of the crowd that lined up for blocks to see the Godfather.

He was never able to leave the scars from his childhood behind. Memories of hunger pangs in Barnwell and Augusta motivated him to provide an annual feast for those who were equally hungry. These were his people. He loved them. Writing that check was easy.

Some families made it through the line twice. It was easy to spot them and some people encouraged my father to withhold his generosity. The thought never crossed his mind. He believed if they needed a second turkey - this was a way for God to provide.

My father loved Christmas. He loved to sing at Christmas and provide hundreds of thousands of dollars in toys for children. He gave back to his community much more than the annual toy giveaway in Augusta. His generosity started back in the 1960s, and never stopped until he died on Christmas day. In particular, he loved to give bicycles to boys and dolls to girls. More importantly, he wanted each child to pick something out that would make them happy. He didn't want their parents or his staff to pick out a toy for them; that was the privilege of the child.

If he ran low on toys or turkeys, he simply turned to his staff and said, "Go buy more, people are still waiting in line." He may have single-handedly saved the toy stores in Augusta.

Danny Ray, his Cape Man said: "Mr. Brown used to give away a lot of things. He would give away toys to kids.

He used to tell me, 'These are things I never had. I never had anything like this. I had to pick cotton in Carolina.' Around Christmas time he would take care of the kids. He knew the kids didn't have a lot of things. If he saw a kid, he would give them whatever he could. He would also try to help the moms. Shoot yeah. He started the Christmas thing because of his memory of being a kid.

It was tough with his daddy thing. He would walk from Barnwell, South Carolina all the way over to Augusta, Georgia. 'More than 50 miles,' he said. 'The first bicycle I got, Glen gave it to me. I rode that bike everywhere.' That is why he gave so many kids bikes. It was better than walking. He also started the toy giveaway. He didn't like to see kids with sad faces. I think he enjoyed watching the kids smile more than even the kid did getting a present.

His Christmas decorations were legendary in Augusta. Thousands of eager spectators drove to see the famous black Santa when he lived up on the hill. What most people don't know - he was Black Santa. He loved to give all year long. He didn't really care if you were naughty or nice; James Brown did not want to see you suffer. He would gladly endure pain for you if he could benefit your life. He never saw color, he only saw need.

It is no coincidence that he died just after the toy giveaway. The thought of this day brought life to a dead man. His life was essentially over as soon as the toy giveaway ended in 2006.

He gave away millions of dollars to the needy during his lifetime. He paid medical bills, rebuilt houses, paid utility bills, and provided hundreds of thousands of dollars in groceries to the needy. He loved to buy school supplies for children. It was his way of telling them to "stay in school."

My father loved to tip big for those who really took care of him. I know he tipped many people ten thousand dollars for their simple service. He loved to take care of single mothers who were waiting tables in restaurants. The money he had was not his. He never hesitated to give back. When he didn't have money, it saddened him. Not because he would go without, but because he could not help others in need. That was the role of the Godfather.

Sadly, Christmas was a time of loneliness and despair for my father. He missed Alphie (heaven only knows why) and he missed the band, his staff, and his friends that were occupied with their families. He was so hard on the band but in an odd way they were his dysfunctional family - the only family he really ever had.

James Brown loved to give his employees a healthy Christmas bonus. Certain years he was not able to provide a bonus - he barely made payroll. This brought about a sense of despair for Mr. "I feel good."

He wanted people to believe in themselves. When he wrote, "Say it loud, I'm black and I'm proud" he was really trying to get his people to "get up on the good foot."

When he saw homeless and unemployed people he became frustrated. It was one thing to be working and poor. It was quite another to simply waste your life away. He said, "Don't give me a handout; give me a way out." He would talk to homeless people in shelters and do what he could to simply get them to move. That was the very essence of his music; it moved body and soul. "Wear your hat in the direction you want your life to go." Move forward not backward.

For the Barnwell High School band, he bought uniforms.

He sent money to Sammy Davis Junior's wife. Davis died in poverty. She became Brown's responsibility. Other entertainers also blessed her life.

My father paid for a young man's college degree. He was one of the very few who showed up at the sentencing of my father in 1989. He wanted to express gratitude. I wish I knew his name - that meant so much to my dad.

My sister Yamma and I have not always been on the same page. She should know that one of the proudest days in my father's life was the day she graduated with her doctorate degree.

He loved to go out for a Wendy's Frosty. They kept him happy. He loved Coca-Cola, he drank way too much soda. He also really enjoyed an Icee. You too can eat like a superstar.

307

I wish you could have seen my father mess with his entourage when they went to a restaurant. He told them what they wanted to eat - and they ordered just as he did.

He loved to eat chicken after church on Sunday.

Every person in this book has a James Brown impression. Their throat gets low and raspy. Al Sharpton and Spike Nealy win the contest.

My father was the king of home remedies. Whatever he bought – he bought by the truckload, and then wanted to make sure everyone around him was taking the very same thing for their health.

He loved to play the lottery. He would drop thousands of dollars each week. He was lucky. I believe he won as much as $75,000.

I was with him when he invested in the stock market. He said, "Watch this Daryl." He made a quick phone call and the stock we were watching moved. He loved that. It made him feel powerful.

He was superstitious. He would throw salt over his left shoulder when he ate. He would cover the TV in his room with a towel or blanket so that people could not watch him. He also thought he was being followed by satellites: Drugs!

He would never do beer commercials. He did not like to drink and was concerned that drinking and driving could cause harm. Really.

He also refused to endorse tennis shoes. He could not stand the thought that kids were killing each other over tennis shoes. He saw that happen in Los Angeles, Atlanta and New York. He thought it was senseless.

He loved a good gun.

I am certain there is still money hidden in hotel rooms where he stayed. He hid it in corners of rooms underneath the carpet. I suspect certain hotels have a pile of cash still hidden to this day. I know he would return to the same hotels year after year. He got a kick out of finding a pile of cash in the same spot. It was like a game to him.

I know my father loved David Cannon and Buddy Dallas. He told me so many times. He would let others believe what they wanted. He knew better - they both saved him.

Michael Jackson called my father every year on his birthday.

My father had no toenails. He lost them dancing in tight shoes for so many years. His feet were a mess.

Doctors terrified him.

I asked my mother why he wore a wig. I always had my hair cut short and tight. I thought all black men had it done that way. It made me laugh to see him underneath the hairdryer getting his hair curled and pressed. He spent hours each day doing his hair. That busted me up.

Buddy Dallas arranged for my father to receive an honorary doctorate degree from Payne University. When he was told, he could hardly speak; one of the few times in his life. The man whose formal education ended with the 7th grade was finally recognized for his genius. He received the award posthumously. It meant more to him than any of the countless awards he received during his lifetime.

Gloria Daniels said he liked the Playboy channel and Westerns. She should have added "The Golden Girls" to that list.

He loved an audience - he loved them hard. They were his one true love.

He loved his parents more than either deserved. He was a gracious enough man to freely forgive.

He was in unbelievable pain during the last six months of his life.

We in the band knew he was no angel – but he was our Superman.

***

I love you Dad.

***

I want to give the last word to his longtime friend, Danny Ray, who recently said:

"I miss him. Oh yeah I miss him. I definitely do. No doubt about it.

Think about him every day. No doubt about it.

Every day was a new adventure with James Brown. It sure was. I would like to think that he's looking out for me.

I sure would."

Daryl Brown

Music icon James Brown's son Daryl Brown was born in
New Brunswick, New Jersey and grew
up with a very clear understanding of
who his father was...James Brown,
The Godfather of Soul. Daryl played
on countless James Brown smash hit
songs and twice toured the world with
his dad. Daryl has appeared on Jay
Leno, David Letterman, BET, MTV and The American
Music Awards to mention a few. Daryl has appeared in
films such as Jackie Chan's "The Tuxedo" and more. Daryl
is an artist, songwriter, musician and producer who is not
just the son of music's most prolific artist, James Brown,
but a shining star in his own right. Daryl took a little time
away after the sudden passing of his father, best friend and
mentor. However, Daryl is ready and poised to take the
world by storm!

Michael P. Chabries

Dr. Michael Chabries is a gifted instructor and talented public speaker. He loves stories and the connections they produce to captivate an audience. Michael spent the first ten years of his professional career in the classroom. The last 12 years have been spent working as a senior political advisor for five remarkable elected officials. Thankfully, he has returned to his roots to teach ethics, leadership and management courses to university students as an adjunct faculty member. *"A boxing match in the fog": leadership, sensemaking and crisis management in the context of an anthrax terrorism environment* is the title of his doctoral dissertation. It is his fervent prayer that one day he will know what those words really mean.

Michael has four beautiful children. His daughter Lauren was recently married and his oldest son Joseph is attending West Point Military Academy.

Catherine is now his favorite child and Christian has a smile that will melt your heart. On a good day, Michael is a poor cyclist but loves to ride nonetheless. The greatest blessing in his life is his wife Laura. For some unknown reason, she continues to love him to this day. Tomorrow might be a different story.

Credits

Photographer: Front cover photo/ artwork giclee by: Kraig Geiger/ Contographer ®/ Concert photographer

Photographer: Back cover photo/ Favoron Productions-Photography. 2014 (Daryl Brown)

Photographer: George Livingston Jr.

Photographer: Robert Braunfeld

Cover Design: Dan and Darlene Swanson

Editor: Jahnavi Newsom